201 Everyday Uses for Salt, Lemons, Vinegar, and Baking Soda

201 EVERYDAY USES FOR

SALT

LEMONS

VINEGAR

AND

BAKING SODA

NATURAL, AFFORDABLE, AND SUSTAINABLE SOLUTIONS FOR THE HOME

BENJAMIN MOTT

SASQUATCH BOOKS

SEATTLE

Printed in the United States of America

SASQUATCH BOOKS with colophon is a registered trademark of Penguin Random House LLC

26 25 24 23 22   9 8 7 6 5 4 3 2 1

Illustrations: Erin Wallace
Editor: Jen Worick
Production editor: Bridget Sweet
Designer: Tony Ong

Library of Congress Cataloging-in-Publication Data

Names: Mott, Benjamin, author.
Title: 201 everyday uses for salt, lemons, vinegar, and baking soda :
  natural, affordable and sustainable solutions for the home / Benjamin
  Mott.
Other titles: Two hundred one everyday uses for salt, lemons, vinegar, and
  baking soda
Description: Seattle, WA : Sasquatch Books, [2022] | Includes index.
Identifiers: LCCN 2022003147 (print) | LCCN 2022003148 (ebook) | ISBN
  9781632174291 (paperback) | ISBN 9781632174307 (epub)
Subjects: LCSH: House cleaning. | Natural products. | Formulas, recipes,
  etc.
Classification: LCC TX324 .M68 2022 (print) | LCC TX324 (ebook) | DDC
  648/.5-dc23/eng/20220213
LC record available at https://lccn.loc.gov/2022003147
LC ebook record available at https://lccn.loc.gov/2022003148

The recipes contained in this book have been created for the ingredients and techniques indicated. Neither publisher nor author is responsible for your specific health or allergy needs that may require supervision. Nor are publisher and author responsible for any adverse reactions you may have to the recipes contained in the book, whether you follow them as written or modify them to suit your personal dietary needs or tastes.

ISBN: 978-1-63217-429-1

Sasquatch Books
1325 Fourth Avenue, Suite 1025
Seattle, WA 98101

SasquatchBooks.com

CONTENTS

CHAPTER 7: The Personal Touch 147

CHAPTER 8: The Animal Kingdom 195

INTRODUCTION
What Have We Gotten Ourselves Into?

Grab any one of the bottles of household cleansers under your sink or in your laundry closet and check out the ingredients—you will be confronted by a Pandora's box of exotic compounds that only a chemical engineer could understand, much less pronounce. Now have a look at the dire words of caution printed on those bottles. Even if you aren't familiar with the chemicals on the ingredients list, are you sure you want something that comes with that kind of warning spread around your home, where you and your loved ones spend most of your sleeping and waking hours?

Of course not! And an excellent way to start detoxing your home is to avoid the commercially made household products that have become more and more common since the early days of the twentieth century. This book provides you with hundreds of simple, natural alternatives to many of the manufactured products we routinely reach for on grocery shelves every time we shop. Not only do these alternatives work just as well as their laboratory-made cousins, they are almost always less expensive.

And much less toxic.

Chances are you decided to pick up this book because you are concerned about the environment and curious about what effect daily human activity—including your own—might have on our planet. Above all, you are holding this book in your hands because you want to do whatever you can to make your home as safe as possible for you and your loved ones. You might also wonder how we as a culture arrived at this position, where products that might not be good for our health are heavily marketed and widely available.

Humankind's ingenuity has led to all sorts of advances that benefit us as individuals and as a society. Leaving aside the troubling question of the unequal global distribution of certain essential resources, the overall abundance of food and material comforts available to us today provides many millions of people around the globe with a lifestyle that would have been inconceivable just one hundred years ago. Unfortunately all that progress has produced side effects for which we were unprepared. Today we are still trying to figure out many of the long-term repercussions.

It was in the nineteenth century that factories began to mass-produce the materials that have made life so much more comfortable and convenient. Unfortunately this also led to the largely indiscriminate dumping of airborne and waterborne waste products—many of them poisonous and long-lasting—that have literally changed the face of the planet. That trend has only accelerated in the decades since then.

In the twentieth century, advances in chemical engineering led to the manufacture of countless exotic compounds that promised (and in many cases, delivered) great benefits. Some were pharmaceuticals that amplified our ability to combat disease. Some were materials-based (one of which yielded one of the single most useful and simultaneously most harmful human inventions: plastic). Some compounds were created for industrial or agricultural applications (like the pesticide DDT). And many others were designed to make life at home easier, whether in preparing and storing food or in cleaning. (By the way, if you have questions about the effects on your health of any chemicals listed as ingredients in your home cleaning or cosmetic products, you can learn more at the Environmental Working Group's excellent website, EWG.org.)

The ecological consequences of global industrialization are still playing out in the broader environment—they're what Superfund sites are made of, after all—so it should come as no surprise that all those waste products have tangible effects in the home too. Did you know, for instance, that before the Industrial Revolution, sterling silver did not tarnish? The dependence on sulfuric acid for many manufacturing processes, but especially in making dyed cloth, introduced large quantities of hydrogen sulfide and sulfur dioxide into the air. And these are two of the chemicals that combine with silver to give it that dull gray-yellow tinge (silver sulfide).

If you learned from your parents or grandparents to make sure your silverware was well covered when storing it, it was to keep these sulfuric compounds from coming into contact with the metal. Alas, such precautions only go so far. As a result it is often necessary to polish silver to wipe away the tarnish before using it. There are three main products commercially available for this purpose: propylene glycol (a viscous ingredient found in many products, including liquid fog and e-cigarettes); sodium carbonate, a white crystalline salt used to make paper, glass, and soap, among other things; and an aluminum silicate–based cream polish.

None of those chemicals are particularly harmful, but they aren't entirely harmless either. Propylene glycol, for instance, is known to trigger asthmatic reactions in people with sensitive lungs and exacerbate eczema; aluminum silicate, while not too toxic if ingested, can be dangerous when inhaled. And there's the fact that these cleaning products come in the type of single-use plastic containers now clogging our oceans and forests.

The good news for your health and your budget is that you can clean your silver flatware and jewelry by combining a few common household ingredients that contain many of the same chemicals: water, salt, baking soda, and aluminum foil. The recipe for this simple solution can be found in **Chapter 2: The Kitchen (page 17)**.

Even as we have learned more about what effects some of these many chemicals have on us, there are many environmental factors that we as individuals simply cannot control. We are forced to rely on corporations and governmental oversight to limit our exposure to them, but because of the financial incentives tangled up in that relationship, we should view these regulatory efforts with some skepticism. Still, we *can* make a meaningful difference in our home lives through careful choices about the foods we purchase and eat (and how we store them), the products we use to keep our houses clean, and the substances we put in and on our bodies.

This book provides hundreds of natural solutions to everyday household cleaning challenges and personal grooming needs. For the most part, you can make these concoctions from different combinations of just four ingredients—salt, lemons, vinegar, and baking soda—in combination with water. Chapter one discusses the chemical properties of these and a few other essential ingredients, explaining in basic terms what makes them so effective. A few other common

ingredients will make guest appearances too. Chapters two through nine contain recipes organized by the area of domestic life where they are most useful.

Ironically, this book represents a return to the wisdom of early Industrial Age homemakers who discovered by necessity (and often without the benefit of scientific research) many ways to combat the environmental stresses of daily life on our homes and on our bodies. Once you start using these simple, affordable, highly effective, convenient, and safe solutions to common household tasks, you may find yourself wondering what took us so long to return to these time-proven methods.

CHAPTER 1

THE
INGREDIENTS

WATER

It may seem strange to begin with a description of one of the most common substances on the planet—it also accounts for around 60 percent of our bodies—but we do need to take a quick moment to celebrate this incredibly useful molecule, made up of just two atoms of hydrogen and one of oxygen.

When astronomers scan other planets and moons for possible signs of life, they always look for evidence of water (usually in the form of ice—it's cold in space). This is because water's ability to act as a solvent—that is, a substance into which other chemicals readily dissolve—makes it foundational in the creation of life. Millions of years of evolution later, most of the chemical processes our bodies perform continue to be possible only because so much of us is composed of water, from our blood to our digestive fluids to our very bones (which themselves are more than one-third aqueous).

When it comes to cleaning, water's ability to dissolve other chemicals is its most important property, which is further enhanced by adding heat. This is why cleaning clothes in hot water is more effective than in cold water, even when no soaps are involved. And when water is boiled, it becomes an excellent disinfectant—the boiling temperature of water (212 degrees F or 100 degrees C) is fatal to most organisms.

Water's ability to dissolve and evenly distribute acids like lemon juice and vinegar, not to mention everyday salt (sodium chloride) and baking soda (sodium bicarbonate, also a salt), make it a staple ingredient in many of the recipes in these pages. This ability derives partly from the fact that the pH level of water is 7 (on a scale of 1 to 14), also referred to as a neutral pH. Lemon juice and vinegar are acids (with a pH below 7), whereas baking soda is a base (with a pH higher than 7). When a recipe calls for distilled water, you can either purchase it or make a suitable alternative by boiling a pot of water for 15 to 20 minutes.

SALT

For the purposes of this book, when we refer to salt we are talking about sodium chloride, a molecule that contains one atom of sodium and one of chloride. It can be found in several different forms in most supermarkets, including **table salt** (enriched with iodine, to promote the health of the thyroid gland, and anticaking agents), **sea salt** (which contains several other minerals in trace amounts, which can add color and flavor), **Epsom salt** (magnesium sulfate), and **kosher salt** (a relatively unprocessed salt with large crystals). The recipes in these pages are all made with non-iodized salt, usually fine sea salt or kosher salt (unless otherwise indicated).

Salt, like water, is one of the most common materials on the planet. In fact, salt is the most abundant nonmetallic mineral in the world, found naturally in the ocean as well as in underground and underwater salt deposits. It is also an essential ingredient in the formation and maintenance of life—without sufficient quantities of salt, we and most other organisms would die. Sodium is vital to brain and muscle function, and chloride is an essential electrolyte. Conversely, in excessive quantities, salt can be fatal, a fact that makes it very useful as a disinfectant—bacteria contain even more water (70 percent) than people do, making them vulnerable to highly saline conditions.

As an essential ingredient in cooking, salt (one of the five basic flavors the human tongue can taste) was for much of recorded history a precious commodity. For that reason it was often taxed, from ancient China (when Emperor Hsia Yu established a salt levy in circa 2200 BCE) to India in 1930, when the onerous salt tax inspired a revolution. The word *salary* itself comes from salt: in ancient Rome, part of the compensation received by the legions was known as *salarium argentum*, the portion of their wage earmarked for the purchase of salt. As Mark Kurlansky put it in his book *Salt: A World History* (2002): "Trade routes that have remained major thoroughfares were established, alliances built, empires secured, and revolutions provoked—all for something that fills the ocean, bubbles up from springs, forms crusts in lake beds, and thickly veins a large part of the earth's rock fairly close to the surface."

Salt has countless uses, from personal to industrial to commercial, though we will mainly focus on its useful properties in cleaning. In its crystalline form, salt can serve as a mild abrasive (good for gently cleaning various surfaces, including the skin). Salt is also highly absorbent, making it useful in removing stains, from wine to blood to sweat (see **Stain Pretreatments, page 132**, for the latter application). And as discussed on the previous page, its antimicrobial properties make it an excellent disinfectant.

LEMONS

Lemons are among the most common citrus fruits in the world, prized for their juice as well as the fragrant oils in their skin. Like all citrus, lemons are native to subtropical and tropical climates, though constant crossbreeding across thousands of years of cultivation makes it hard to pinpoint exactly where they got their start. As a result of all this cultivation, today many varieties of lemon are available around the world, each prized for its unique flavor. In North America the most common by far is the Eureka lemon, grown in California and Florida.

Like salt, lemons were a treasured commodity, carried by Arab traders along early trade routes that stretched from the foothills of the Himalayas to the Middle East and Africa. They then found their way to what is now southern Italy around the year 200 CE (and then spread to the rest of Europe). Unlike salt, however, lemons were not originally used for cooking—instead, they were treasured as ornamental trees and prized for their fragrance. It wasn't until the fifteenth century that lemons began to be widely used in the kitchen.

As overland trade routes were replaced by nautical ones, both salt and lemons became vitally important on the sailing ships that crisscrossed the world in the eighteenth and nineteenth centuries. Salt was prized as a way to preserve meat in the era before refrigeration, making monthslong voyages possible. And lemons and other citrus fruits became staples when it was discovered that eating them prevented scurvy, a dreadful disease that had long plagued ships' crews. In 1747, a Scotsman named James Lind, a ship's surgeon serving aboard the British navy vessel *HMS Salisbury*, conducted one of the first known controlled clinical trials in history, proving conclusively that a regular diet of citrus fruits prevented scurvy. (In 1928 it was discovered that the disease results from an insufficient supply of vitamin C, also known as ascorbic acid.)

But since this is not a cookbook (or a first-aid guide for sailors), we celebrate lemons for the fragrant oils in their rinds and the cleaning powers of their juice, mainly thanks to its citric acid. As a mildly acidic (low pH) organic compound, the citric acid in lemon juice is useful as a cleaning agent and disinfectant and can be used to whiten fabrics, ceramics, and even some plastics, and to lighten hair (see **Hair Color Lightener, page 169**). And since its scent is so delightful and invigorating, lemon juice makes an excellent addition to many cleaning solutions.

VINEGAR

Like lemon juice, vinegar is an essential cleaning agent thanks to its high acidity (or low pH). The strength of the acetic acid in a given vinegar depends on the amount of water added to the acid to dilute it—most vinegars sold at supermarkets have a concentration of about 5 percent. Concentrations above 10 percent make the vinegar more dangerous to handle but also that much more effective against tough-to-tackle cleaning jobs like mineral deposits. For the purposes of this book, *vinegar* means **white vinegar** in a full-strength, conventional 5 percent solution unless otherwise indicated (as, for instance, the recipe for **Fruit Fly Trap, page 52**, which uses apple cider vinegar).

Vinegar is produced by a natural process of double fermentation. In the first step, sugars in a mash of fruit or grain are consumed by yeast, which then excrete alcohol in the form of ethanol. (This is how wine and beer are made too.) In the second step, *Acetobacter* bacteria consume the ethanol and excrete acetic acid. To accomplish this, the bacteria require oxygen, which is why vinegar production occurs in open-air containers. Over the centuries, humans have experimented widely with different grains and fruits to create many types of vinegars, including **balsamic vinegar**, **rice vinegar**, **malt vinegar**, and **wine vinegars** of countless varieties.

Vinegar is a common substance found in every human community on Earth. Mentions of vinegar exist as far back as the earliest recorded history, appearing in Babylonian scrolls dating to 5000 BCE that identify it as useful in preserving food. Traces of vinegar itself were found in Egyptian urns that date to around 3000 BCE. The father of modern medicine, the ancient Greek physician Hippocrates, records using vinegar to treat the wounds of his patients around 420 BCE. Vinegar is given a shout-out in the *Zuo Zhuan*, the oldest work of Chinese narrative history (covering the period from roughly 770 to 475 BCE), as an essential ingredient in a harmoniously balanced fish soup. The Bible refers to vinegar both as a food and as a medicine. Vinegar's use in scientific applications became widespread through the centuries, and the tenth-century Chinese forensic scientist Sung Tse recommended using it in combination with sulfur as an antiseptic handwash to prevent infection during autopsies. Accounts of vinegar as an ingredient in cooking, cleaning, and medicine are ubiquitous in records from the Middle Ages to today.

As a household product, vinegar's uses are numerous. Beyond its culinary applications, it can be used to safely clean many different surfaces, from textiles to ceramic tile to finished wood (though not natural stone), all thanks to its acidity. It has powerful antiseptic properties too, which makes it useful as a disinfectant.

BAKING SODA

As a kid, when I first heard of baking soda, I was convinced it was a carbonated sweet beverage designed to make cooks feel better about having to slave away in a hot kitchen. As an adult, I have come to appreciate that it is a miraculous addition to the baker's toolkit, making it possible to leaven baked goods without the use of yeast, as well as a boon to home cleaning and deodorizing.

Baking soda, or sodium bicarbonate, is found in a white crystalline mineral named nahcolite (so-called because of the letters of the atoms of which it is composed: sodium, or NA; hydrogen; carbon; and oxygen). It can be mined, where it is found in association with a mineral called trona, or it can be manufactured in a laboratory. Today most baking soda around the world is made in factory labs, but in a few countries (including the United States) it is still mined.

References to related compounds stretch back as far as ancient Egypt, where sodium carbonate was used to preserve the mummified remains of the rich and famous. By the eighteenth century, American bakers were toying with similar chemicals (like potassium carbonate, also known as pearl ash) as a way of reliably leavening baked goods without finicky yeast or other labor-intensive methods (such as whipping a bunch of egg whites every time you baked a cake). In 1791, a French chemist named Nicolas Leblanc derived a method for creating sodium carbonate, or soda ash, in a lab. But in 1801, a German pharmacologist named Valentin Rose the Younger did him one carbonate better and developed sodium bicarbonate for the first time. By the beginning of the twentieth century, bakers everywhere celebrated this widely available and magical substance, which released bubbles of carbon dioxide when exposed to heat, making cakes and spirits rise around the world.

Then, in 1970, an interesting event occurred that brought widespread attention to the wondrous cleaning properties of baking soda. That year the Arm & Hammer company, which was created in 1846 and made its fortune thanks in part to baking soda, became the sole sponsor of the very first Earth Day celebration, during which the use of sodium bicarbonate as a safe, nontoxic alternative to harsh, commercial cleaning agents was championed. And this brings us to its starring role in this book.

Baking soda is useful for cleaning for a few important reasons. It's a base (with a pH of 9), which makes it good at breaking up organic compounds, especially in combination with (low pH) acids like vinegar or lemon juice. This combination causes the baking soda to foam (as any elementary school kid who has made a "working volcano" can tell you), the action of which can loosen stuck-on grime. Plus baking soda is gently abrasive, making it perfect as a scrubbing salt for even very delicate surfaces. And finally, because most scents are acidic molecules, baking soda acts as a powerful neutralizer to those odors, giving it its remarkable odor-eating qualities.

OLIVE OIL

Olive oil is, or should be, a staple in any kitchen—it is a healthy, natural fat extracted from the small, oval fruit of the olive tree. Not only is it delicious, it is also very good for you. The health benefits of the so-called Mediterranean diet (including low incidences of heart disease and diabetes, and a reduced likelihood of many kinds of cancer) are widely believed to result from the prevalence of olive oil in the region's cuisines.

Not surprisingly, the history of olive oil is the history of much of civilization, including northern Africa, Asia Minor, and western and southern Europe. Anthropologists have uncovered evidence that olive trees were domesticated in the eastern Mediterranean as far back as 8,000 to 6,000 years ago, near modern-day Turkey and Syria. The exact location is a matter of some debate, but it is safe to say the spread of cultivated olive trees happened in parallel with the spread of the local populations, eventually extending to every corner of the Mediterranean basin.

Mentions of the olive abound in ancient literature, from the works of the ancient Greeks, who believed it was a gift of Athena, to the Bible, where it appears as a symbol of peace. In addition to their trademark purple dye, Phoenician traders sold olive oil widely throughout the eastern reaches of the Mediterranean for hundreds of years. Reports of olive oil can be found in accounts of the Roman Republic, and in the age of the Roman Empire the cultivation of the tree was broadened even farther by conquering legions as they fanned out across Europe and Africa. By some accounts, the quantity of olive oil the Romans produced at one point would not be matched again until the nineteenth century. In the early 1500s, in the wake of the Columbian Exchange, monks and explorers who followed the Spanish conquistadors brought tree cuttings with them, spreading olive cultivation to the Americas.

Although primarily thought of as a foodstuff, olive oil has many other uses outside of cooking, from personal care to home maintenance to cleaning. The ancient Greeks and Romans used it to clean their bodies after exercise. It was used as an ingredient in perfumes, an all-purpose lubricant (as useful in the smooth operation of wooden machinery as it was for providing massages), a fuel in lamps, and a religious offering.

The highest-quality olive oil (and also the most expensive) is called **extra-virgin**, which means extracted from the first pressing of the olives, with no heat added ("cold-pressed"). This grade of oil has the greatest health benefits, including many antioxidants, and the best aroma and flavor. From there the grades are, in descending

ESSENTIAL OILS: WHAT THEY ARE
AND HOW TO USE THEM SAFELY

Many of the recipes in this book call for the addition of various essential oils, in some cases for their scent and in others for their therapeutic properties. They are called "essential" because they contain the *essence* of the plants from which they are made. Depending on the plant source, the method of extraction of these volatile compounds varies: some are distilled, for instance, while others might be gathered by cold-pressing (that is, crushing them at room temperature to avoid damaging the delicate phytochemicals) or by adding a solvent (such as alcohol). Whatever the extraction method, the result is a highly concentrated liquid that can be used in tiny amounts to impart a robust aroma to your creations.

Before you purchase essential oils, it's important to do your homework. This is a growing market that is not subject to government regulation, so there are lots of unscrupulous purveyors out there selling low-quality essential oils, some of which are made from synthetic ingredients. The most reputable essential-oil producers

order: **virgin olive oil**, **olive oil**, **olive pomace oil**, and **lampante** (a low-grade oil that has no culinary value but does have many other applications). For the purposes of the recipes in this book, your budget should be your guide, but in general it is not necessary to use a delicate, flavorful, and expensive extra-virgin olive oil for anything that doesn't go into or onto your body. I recommend using the lowest-possible grade of olive oil, which has little to no odor and no particulates, for cleaning applications, and the highest grade for homemade cosmetics. While you'll spend more on high-end olive oils, those prices are nowhere near the cost of high-end cosmetics.

generally have their products certified as genuine by third-party labs and make the test results available on their websites.

Because of their concentrated nature, essential oils must be handled carefully. Undiluted, many of these substances can cause contact dermatitis (especially if you have sensitive skin). Tea tree, lemongrass, ylang-ylang, peppermint, and clove essential oils, for instance, are well-known to cause skin irritation at full strength. Before using any essential oil that will be in contact with your (or your pet's) skin, apply a little diluted oil to a small area and wait a few moments to see if a rash develops. To dilute an essential oil, mix **a couple drops** into **a tablespoon (15 mL) of a carrier oil** (**olive or coconut oil** work well) rather than a water-based liquid. Additionally, **be careful with diffusion—some oils, such as pine and citrus, can be toxic to pets**.

Finally, **never ingest an essential oil**—despite smelling heavenly, some of them can cause serious complications if taken orally. And while it is true that some are used in trace amounts in food manufacturing (the US Food and Drug Administration's website, FDA.gov, includes the Food Additive Status List, which contains information about food-safe essential oils), in general you should avoid ingesting these liquids.

OTHER USEFUL NATURAL INGREDIENTS

Activated charcoal powder. This jet-black, ultrafine, odorless powder is produced by superheating (carbonizing) wood or other carbon-rich fuel. It is very useful for its ability to absorb chemicals and odors of all kinds.

Aloe vera. One of some five hundred similar species of the genus *Aloe*, this desert succulent is prized for the cooling, viscous fluid flowing through its fronds. Its use in treating skin conditions extends back to roughly 4000 BCE. Clinical studies of its efficacy are scant, but it is recommended for various topical and internal ailments, and is acknowledged to have powerful antibacterial, antiviral, and antifungal properties. It is available in gel and liquid form.

Argan oil. Derived from the kernels of the argan tree, which is native to Morocco, this delicious oil is rich in vitamins and antioxidants. In this book, argan oil is primarily reserved for cosmetic recipes, mainly because it is more expensive than other oils due to its arduous extraction process.

Beeswax. Honeybees produce beeswax to build the honeycomb structures that protect their honey and their larvae. It is edible but more useful for a variety of nonculinary purposes: as a waterproofing material, lubricant, candle wax, wood and leather polish, and in cosmetics manufacturing. When buying beeswax, try to buy ethically sourced products—honeybee populations around the world are under immense stress.

Coconut oil. Available in virgin and refined forms, this wonderfully silky oil is useful in countless ways, from cooking to cosmetics to cleaning. In this book, the recipes call for virgin coconut oil, which is minimally processed and smells like its namesake ingredient (whereas refined coconut oil is almost odorless).

Cornstarch. A finely ground powder made from grains of corn, cornstarch has a variety of uses in the kitchen, in industrial applications (like glue-making), in medicine, in textile manufacturing, and in cosmetics. Cornstarch is so fine it is silky to the touch, but it is especially prized because when it is mixed with water and heated, it becomes a flavorless, transparent gel.

Herbs and spices. The use of herbs and spices in homemade cleaning and cosmetic products opens up a universe of scents and therapeutic properties. Both fresh and dried herbs and spices feature in numerous recipes in these pages.

Honey. Made by bees in the genus *Apis,* honey is the first and perhaps greatest superfood. This golden, viscous liquid is delicious, loaded with vitamins and minerals, and antibacterial, making it useful in treating wounds and fighting illness.

Hydrogen peroxide. First manufactured in the late eighteenth century, it is used today for commercial purposes in the bleaching of paper pulp. In the domestic sphere it is sold in concentrations of around 5 percent as a bleaching agent in cleaning and cosmetic treatments, and as a topical disinfectant. Because it breaks down into oxygen and water, it is considered environmentally friendly.

Isopropyl alcohol. First manufactured in 1920 by Standard Oil, this powerful solvent is distilled from an organic compound called propene. It is a powerful antiseptic and appears in this book mainly in that role. Most of the recipes call for a concentration of 70 percent, which can be diluted to lower concentrations by adding water.

Liquid Castile soap. Castile soap is a vegetable oil–based soap that has been around for millennia. Effective as a surfactant and prized for its purity, this ancient style of soap contains no animal by-products and is nontoxic and completely biodegradable.

Milk. For the purposes of this book, *milk* refers to cow's milk and is used for its skin-nourishing properties, which stem from its high fat and protein content.

Oats. A grain with many beneficial properties when eaten, oats are also prized for their ability to soothe irritated skin.

Pure witch hazel extract. Witch hazels belong to a genus (*Hamamelis*) of deciduous shrubs native to North America, China, and Japan. Made from a distillation of the flowers, leaves, and bark, the extract is prized for its astringent qualities, thanks to the presence of tannic acid. When buying extract, purchase the alcohol-free variety.

Tea. Made from the same leaves but processed differently, black tea and green tea contain numerous beneficial chemicals, including tannin (an astringent acid) and various antioxidants, which help promote cellular health. Herbal teas are made from a huge variety of herbs and flowers that, depending on the ingredients, also have numerous health benefits.

TOOLS OF THE TRADE

This is a short list of some of the equipment mentioned in the pages of this book. If you are committed to making your own environmentally friendly, all-natural products, you will need a wide variety of these items.

- Spray bottles in various sizes, preferably glass
- Glass dropper bottles of various sizes
- Small and medium glass jars
- Small and large funnels
- Small, medium, and large bowls
- Plastic buckets (at least two)
- Pump sprayer (64 ounces)
- Empty sachets

- Lint-free cloths
- Microfiber cloths
- Cotton balls and cotton swabs
- Sponges (with and without scouring pads) and dry mops
- Long-handled scrub brush
- Brooms
- Vacuum cleaner

CHAPTER 2

THE KITCHEN

Perhaps the most time-worn cliché about the kitchen is that it is
the heart of the home—but like most clichés, it is uttered so often
because it's true. The kitchen is where we wind up spending a lot
of our waking hours, preparing meals, grabbing snacks, eating and
drinking, and just hanging out. And because it often has a door that
leads outside—or is situated close to the entrance to the home,
whether a house or an apartment—the kitchen is also a heavily
trafficked thoroughfare. Due to all this activity, much of it quite
messy, the kitchen probably sees the hardest use of any room in the
house. The recipes in this chapter will help combat the chaos.

All-Purpose Cleanser

Every cleaning arsenal requires a multipurpose cleanser capable of handling a wide variety of household cleaning challenges, from dirty stovetops to coffee tables, grease-stained clothing to bathroom sinks, and car interiors to most countertops (but not natural stone, many types of which are easily damaged by acids such as vinegar; see **Natural Stone Countertop Cleanser, page 25**, for this type of surface). This simple preparation makes a great-smelling, highly effective cleaning solution for countless situations.

NOTE: If you're in need of a glass cleaner, see **All-Purpose Glass Cleaner (page 70)**.

~~~~~~~~~

- Mix **3 large strips of lemon peel** with **2 cups (500 mL) white vinegar** in a **glass jar with a tight-fitting lid**. Let this mixture stand for **4 weeks**, giving it a good shake every couple of days.

- Strain the mixture through a **fine-mesh stainless-steel strainer or cheesecloth** and pour into a **clean 16-ounce (500 mL) glass spray bottle**.

NOTE: If you don't have time to wait for the lemon peels to steep, substitute **5 to 10 drops lemon essential oil**; the spray will be ready to use immediately.

Stainless-Steel Cleaner

Anyone with stainless-steel appliances knows how difficult it is to keep them clean—stainless steel shows fingerprints and other stains, but cleaning it with soap leaves an unsightly film behind. This simple solution takes advantage of baking soda's mild abrasive qualities to make an effective cleaner that leaves no residue.

- Add **1 heaping tablespoon (15 mL) baking soda** to the surface of a **clean, damp sponge**. Holding it over the sink, squeeze the sponge to release enough moisture into the baking soda to create a thick paste. Rub the paste onto the surfaces you are cleaning in wide circles. Rinse the sponge and wring it out, and wipe the surfaces clean with the damp sponge. Buff with a **clean, lint-free cloth**.

Copper Cleaner

Copper cookware is much loved by cooks everywhere—the metal is famously conductive, heating evenly and quickly, and it looks stunning. All this comes at a cost though: copper pots, pans, and bowls are very expensive and, because the metal tarnishes easily, require a lot of maintenance. Luckily you probably have the necessary ingredients for an excellent cleaner in your home right now. Oh, and don't forget to polish your brass too (antique door handles, I'm looking at you)—brass is an alloy of copper and zinc, so this solution works just as well on all those doorknobs and sculptures.

* Cut **1 lemon** in half and wrap each half in a **small piece of cheesecloth**. (No cheesecloth? No problem—it works almost as well without it.) Sprinkle **1½ teaspoons (7.5 mL) of salt** on each cut surface of lemon and use that side to polish your **copper cookware**. Add a little more salt as you go, as needed. Rinse and thoroughly dry with a **dish towel**.

Silver Polish

Silver flatware and dinnerware are among the most prized possessions in any home, passed down from generation to generation and trotted out for special occasions. Because of all the sulfurous chemicals that have been released into the environment since the Industrial Revolution, however, this beautiful metal tarnishes easily. Many consumer products have been developed to keep silver looking its best, but you have everything you need to clean it right now. (By the way, this works just as well on silver jewelry.)

● Heat **2 quarts (2 L) water** to a **boil** and pour into a **large, wide bowl**. Stir in **1 cup (250 mL) baking soda** until incorporated, then add a **2-inch (5 cm) by 12-inch (60 cm) strip of aluminum foil.** Lay the **silverware** (and **dinnerware** that is small enough to fit) into the bowl and soak for at least **30 minutes**.

● In a **small bowl**, prepare a mixture of **¾ cup (180 mL) baking soda and ¼ cup (60 mL) water**. As you remove each piece of silverware from the large bowl, apply a small amount of the baking soda paste and rub thoroughly with a **clean, lint-free cloth**. Then wash the silverware by hand with mild soap, rinse, and dry.

Chrome Polish

Chrome faucets and other fixtures are in constant use, and in the kitchen that often means by hands covered in flour, sugar, or other cooking ingredients. But even if you're a neat freak, never fear. When the task at hand is done, it's a snap to polish up those fixtures.

- Dampen a **lint-free cloth** with a small quantity of **white vinegar** and use the soaked cloth to polish your **chrome fixtures**. Afterward, polish the fixtures with a **separate, dry cloth**.

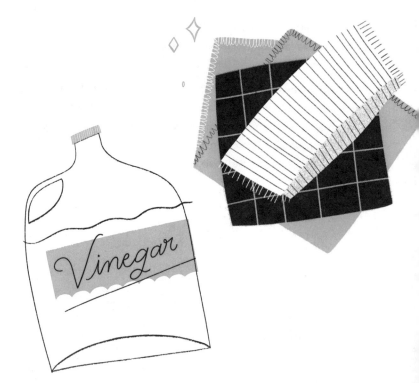

Pewter Polish

Pewter is an ancient metal with a warm, dark luster, used by the Egyptians and later the Romans and others to make all kinds of flatware and dinnerware. By the Middle Ages, pewter was the most widely used material in Europe for such items, only to be replaced by the introduction of commercially produced glassware and ceramic in the eighteenth and nineteenth centuries. Pewter is a soft alloy made of tin, antimony, copper, bismuth, and other metals in trace amounts. While it looks lovely, a word of caution: For much of its history, pewter was also made with lead, a neurotoxin. **Any antique pewter ware should be for display only and never be used for drinking or eating.**

- To liven up the patina of your **pewter ware**, sprinkle **½ teaspoon (2.5 mL) olive oil** onto a **lint-free cloth** and use it to polish the surface of the metal. As the cloth picks up the tarnish, sprinkle more olive oil onto another section and continue until your pewter is glowing.

Cutting Board and Countertop Disinfectant

Pity the poor cutting board—not only does it see every manner of cooking ingredient, it also has to suffer the indignity of being hacked at with knives. Cutting boards should be cleaned after every use to discourage the development of unwanted smells and to prevent the growth of bacteria and other potentially harmful pathogens in the scarred surface. This also goes for any non-stone countertops. But why use harsh commercial cleansers when you can whip up an entirely effective and nontoxic alternative?

- In a **small bowl**, make a paste by mixing **2 tablespoons (30 mL) lemon juice** and **2 tablespoons (30 mL) salt**. Then, using a **clean, lint-free cloth or paper towel**, apply the paste all over both sides of the **cutting board** and let sit for **5 minutes** before thoroughly rinsing with water and drying the board.

NOTE: To condition your **wooden cutting boards** and protect them from splitting or warping, dip a **clean, lint-free cloth or paper towel** in **olive oil** and rub into the surface of the wood after rinsing and drying.

Natural Stone Countertop Cleanser

Natural stone countertops are a beauty to behold and have many other excellent qualities, especially their ability to stay cooler than the ambient temperature (a feature much loved by pastry chefs). However, many types of stone can easily be damaged by acids (which have a low pH), so vinegar and lemon juice are both no-no's when cleaning granite, marble, and so on. Unfortunately these natural materials are also damaged by bases (which have a high pH) such as baking soda and the chlorine bleach found in many commercial cleaners. A safe cleanser should be as close to neutral pH as possible. If you have a lot of stone in your home, whether in the kitchen or in the bathroom, consider making a dedicated batch of this cleanser and storing it in a spray bottle.

- In a **clean 32-ounce (1 L) glass spray bottle**, mix together **1 cup (250 mL) 70 percent isopropyl alcohol**, **2½ cups (625 mL) water**, **1 teaspoon (5 mL) Castile soap**, and **10 drops essential oil of your choice**. Screw the nozzle onto the bottle and gently swirl the mixture until it is evenly mixed. To use, spray onto your **stone countertop, floor, or backsplash,** and wipe it up with a **clean, damp, lint-free cloth or clean, damp sponge**.

Broom Bristle Preserver

Straw brooms are useful items in any home, but the bristles can become brittle and break with heavy use. To get the most mileage out of your new straw broom (or to extend the life of an existing broom), follow these simple instructions before its next use and the bristles will last much longer. Repeat the process **every six months**.

- In a **bucket** large enough to submerge the entire head of the broom, make a saline solution by combining **½ cup (125 mL) salt** for every **1 quart (1 L) warm water**.

- Completely submerge the **head of the broom** in the salty water for **30 minutes**, then remove and dry thoroughly before use. The cells of the bristles will be tightened by the salt, making them more resilient.

Kitchen Sponge Disinfectant

Ah, the kitchen sponge—it sees things in daily use that would make most of us recoil in horror. Sponges do hard labor in the kitchen, becoming impregnated with tiny bits of food and grime, all of which foster the growth of bacteria. This can lead to odors that are then transferred to the objects you are cleaning. By using this simple procedure **once or twice per week**, you will keep your sponges clean and fresh for far longer.

● In a **large bowl**, combine **¼ cup (75 g) salt** with **1 quart (1 L) warm water**, stirring to combine. Soak any dirty, smelly **sponges** in the water **overnight**, weighing them down with a ceramic or other nonreactive small plate to keep them submerged. In the morning, those sponges will once again be clean and smelling their very best.

Ceramic Sink Cleanser

Ceramic sinks are beautiful, but you need to treat them gently to maintain their good looks. Use this simple preparation for a scrub that will keep your ceramic sink looking its best.

- In a **small bowl**, make a paste of **1 tablespoon (15 mL) baking soda** and **1 teaspoon (5 mL) lemon juice**. Apply the frothy mixture to a **clean, damp sponge** and scour the **sink** before rinsing both the sink and the sponge with **warm water**. Add **2 tablespoons (30 mL) white vinegar** to the clean, damp sponge and go over the sink again to thoroughly disinfect it. Finally, rinse the sink with water to remove any remaining cleanser.

Oven Cleanse

One of the most unwelcome, and most often avoided, household tasks is cleaning the oven. As dishes cook under high heat, the ingredients bubble and splash, coating the walls of the oven with sticky, baked-on grime. Lots of commercially made compounds can be used to clean this heat-forged mess, but you already have everything you need on hand to scour your oven.

NOTE: Your first step should be to run the oven-cleaning cycle. Make sure to open nearby windows and turn on the vent above the stove before you do—there *will* be smoke. Let the oven cool before cleansing.

- Begin by emptying the **oven** of anything not permanently affixed to its walls, including the racks, which should be cleaned separately.

- In a **medium bowl**, mix **1 heaping cup (250 mL) baking soda** with **½ cup (125 mL) water** to create a paste—if it seems a little thick, add another **tablespoon (15 mL) water**, a few drops at a time, until you get a spreadable consistency. Wearing **gloves**, spread **about half the paste** all over the walls of the oven with your fingers, being careful not to get any on the heating elements. Don't forget the inside of the oven door, window included. Let it sit at least **2 hours**, or until dry.

- While the paste is lifting the grime in the oven, **spread some of the remaining mixture** onto a **sponge** or **scouring pad**. In the sink, rub down the ribs of the **oven racks** with the paste, reapplying as necessary. When you're done, rinse thoroughly and set aside to dry.

- After the 2 hours have passed, take your spray bottle of **All-Purpose Cleanser (page 18)** and spray the inside of the oven to activate the now-dried paste, which will begin to foam. Again wearing **gloves**, rub a **damp, lint-free cloth** over the inside of the oven to remove all of the remaining residue, rinsing and wringing the cloth in a **bucket of warm water** as necessary. Finally, replace the racks.

Grease Fire Control

Every now and then—and thankfully, this rarely happens—a dish cooked with oil or fat will catch fire when the flames from the stovetop lick over the edge of the pan and ignite the grease. When this happens, it is important to stay calm and put out the fire before it spreads to the hood of the oven or nearby cabinets.

● The first thing to know is that you should **never, ever try to put out a grease fire with water or flour**. If you add water to a grease fire, it will explode, sending flaming droplets of oil throughout the kitchen, and flour is itself flammable. If the fire is small, pour **1 to 2 cups (250 to 500 mL) salt or baking soda** over it to douse the flames. If the fire is more sizable, place a baking sheet over the flaming pan to smother the flames. If the fire persists, evacuate immediately and call 911 once you're a safe distance away.

Refrigerator Cleanse

Refrigerators are the "safe spaces" of any kitchen, the place where leftovers go to fight another day and where milk stays drinkable, often past its suggested shelf life. Of course spills happen in there too, and tend to go unaddressed longer than they would, for instance, on your counter. Luckily there is a safe, effective way to prevent the fridge from losing its rep as a clean, well-lit (at least, when the door is open) place.

- In a **small bowl**, mix ¼ cup (60 mL) salt with ¼ cup (60 mL) **baking soda** until well incorporated. Remove the items from the **refrigerator shelf** and use a spoon to sprinkle a liberal quantity of the mixture on any spills or stubborn stains.

- One at a time, spray the mounds of salt and baking soda with a shot from the **All-Purpose Cleanser (page 18)** to activate the mixture. Then, using a **damp sponge** and a **small bucket of hot water**, start scrubbing. When all the stains are gone, dry the shelf with a **lint-free cloth**.

Refrigerator Deodorizer

This is perhaps the most common non-baking use of baking soda, made possible by the powder's odor-eating superpowers. As you will see in many other recipes in this book (including **Trash Can and Recycling Bin Deodorizer, page 34**), this odor-absorbing property will be put to good use in a number of other smelly trouble spots around the home.

- Completely remove the top of a **small box of baking soda** (the more surface area exposed the better) and place it at the back of a shelf in your **refrigerator or freezer**. After **2 months**, the baking soda will lose its ability to soak up odors and should be replaced. Don't throw it out, however—it will continue to be useful for making many of the cleaning solutions in this book where odor is not an issue (including the **Oven Cleanse, page 29**). But whatever you do, don't bake with it unless you're making, say, Refrigerator Flavored Sponge Cake.

Refrigerator and Freezer Freshener

If, in addition to deodorizing your refrigerator, you'd like to *add in* a pleasant odor, look no further than this simple trick, which accomplishes the same thing for your icebox that the scented cutout of the pine tree hanging from your rearview mirror does for your car.

- Dampen **3 to 5 cotton balls** in **lemon juice** (or add **3 drops lemon essential oil**) and add **1 scented cotton ball** to each **shelf** and **produce drawer** in your **refrigerator**. Do not add any cotton balls to your dairy or meat drawers, though, since you don't want an overlay of lemon scent on those items.

- Soak a **clean, damp sponge** in **lemon juice**, wring out the excess, and swab the "lobby" of your **freezer**—the 2 inches (5 cm) or so around the opening—with the lemon-scented sponge.

Trash Can and Recycling Bin Deodorizer

In a way, the trash can is the armpit of the kitchen, a receptacle highly susceptible to the growth of bacteria that cause bad smells. As with all the other deodorizing tips and recipes in this book, it's baking soda to the rescue.

NOTE: This treatment is effective in **bathroom and bedroom trash cans** too, so feel free to tackle the armpits of every room in the house.

~~~~~~~~~~

- To keep your trash receptacles from stinking up the place, sprinkle a **thin layer of baking soda** at the bottom of the **bin once per week**, making sure to **vacuum** up the previous sprinkling before you do.

- If you'd like a pro solution to the stinky can problem, consider creating scented baking soda and storing it in a dedicated shaker. First, find a **clean jam jar** or similar container and **poke holes in the screw-on metal lid** with a **hammer and nail**. Add **1 cup (250 mL) baking soda** and **15 to 20 drops essential oil** (I recommend **lemon, lavender, or peppermint**) to the jar and use a **fork** to thoroughly incorporate. Put the lid back on and voilà—your scented garbage can deodorant shaker is primed and ready to go.

Garbage Disposal Refresher

The garbage disposal is one of the handiest, and easily the most terrifying, appliance in any kitchen. The sound and fury of the whirring blades converting a load of food scraps into a slurry beneath the sink is the stuff of horror movies. And when you consider that it eats most of your produce waste several times per day, it's no wonder this monster's mouth needs a good cleaning and a breath freshener every now and then.

- With the disposal and the water turned off, pour **½ cup (125 mL) baking soda** down the drain and follow it with a **1-cup (500 mL) chaser of white vinegar**. Roughly **5 minutes later**, when this mixture has finished foaming, drop **two halves of a fresh lemon** down the drain, turn on the water, and awaken the beast. Let the water and disposal run for **1 minute**.

Dishwasher Cleanse

It may seem counterintuitive to clean an appliance that is, itself, designed to clean your dishes, but if you want those dishes to come out looking (and smelling) their best, that's exactly what you need to do. Since most dishes go into the dishwasher with at least some food on them, it makes sense that over time some food debris will build up. Add to that minerals left behind by "hard" water (which passes through limestone, gypsum, or chalk to get to your local water system), detergent residue, and the occasional jar label, and it's easy to see why your dishwasher sometimes needs to be washed too. Depending on usage, you should clean your dishwasher every **one to six months**.

- First, **remove the upper and lower racks**, including any **silverware baskets**, and place them in your sink. In a **small bowl**, mix together **1 tablespoon (15 mL) baking soda** and **2 teaspoons (10 mL) water** to create a thick paste. Spread **1 teaspoon (5 mL) of this mixture** onto a **damp sponge** and rub down the ribs of the dishwasher racks and silverware baskets, reapplying as necessary. When you're done, rinse thoroughly and set aside.

- Next, spray down the **gasket** that lines the door with **All-Purpose Cleanser (page 18)** and scrub along the length of the gasket with an **old, soft toothbrush or non-scouring sponge** to remove any sticky buildup. Immediately rinse the gasket with **warm water** to remove any remaining vinegar, which (because it is an acid) can damage the gasket itself.

- Spray the **inside walls**, including **inside the door**, with the All-Purpose Cleanser and wipe down the interior with a **damp sponge**, paying attention to the corners and cracks where grime can hide. **The area around the filter**, which sits below the lower spray arm, is especially prone to buildup, so you may want to use an old toothbrush here too.

- The **filter** itself should be cleaned at least every **six months**—if it is filled with gunk, your so-called clean dishes will be gunked up too. Following the instructions for your dishwasher (though usually it's pretty self-explanatory), unlock and remove the **filter basket** and rinse it clean in the sink with **warm water**. **Do not scrub the filter with a sponge**, as you may damage it—instead, use the spray nozzle on your sink to blast out any grime.

- Replace the filter, both racks, and the silverware basket and then place a **small bowl** with **1 cup (250 mL) white vinegar** in the top rack. Run the dishwasher on a regular cycle.

Dishwasher Soap

Like most cleaning products, commercial dishwasher soaps contain a long list of ingredients that can include coloring agents, phosphates (used to soften water and prevent limescale, these compounds have been classified as a health hazard), enzymes, bleaching agents, surfactants (which break up grease and oil), perfumes, gelling agents for liquid soaps (or anticaking agents for solid soaps), and a host of other chemicals. But even the toughest post-meal mess can be cleaned from your plates, glasses, and silverware using this simple, environmentally friendly, nontoxic, and inexpensive soap.

● In a **medium bowl**, combine **½ cup (125 mL) liquid Castile soap, 3 tablespoons (45 mL) baking soda**, and **3 tablespoons (45 mL) salt**. Add **½ cup (125 mL) water** and gently stir using a **wire whisk** to make a thick paste (don't worry if it's slightly lumpy). Using a **silicone spatula or bowl scraper**, transfer the paste to a **disposable pastry bag fitted with a wide tip or to a resealable plastic sandwich bag with a ¼-inch (6 mm) triangle snipped from one corner**. Squeeze the dishwasher paste into a **12-ounce (375 mL) plastic squeeze bottle**. To use, squirt **1 to 2 tablespoons (15 to 30 mL) dishwasher soap** (depending on the size and grime factor of the load) into the detergent cup of the dishwasher.

Homemade Rinse Agent

One of life's minor disappointments is when you run the
dishwasher, only to find that your glassware is still foggy or spotty
instead of sparkling clean. This is a result of mineral and detergent
residue, which is unavoidable but easily remedied. This recipe
provides a simple, homemade solution that will save you the cost
and trouble of buying a commercial rinse agent.

● In a **small, clean, resealable jar**, add **1 drop natural blue
food dye** to enough **white vinegar** to fill the jar. Whenever your
dishwasher's **rinse agent cup** runneth dry, add your homemade
rinse agent to fill (which you will be able to see, thanks to the blue
color, in the rinse agent window).

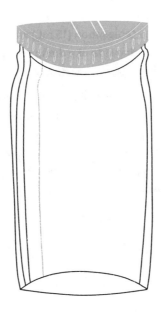

Microwave Steam Cleanse

Microwave technology was developed after World War II, based on the then relatively new radar technology that had helped the Allies win the war. But microwave ovens weren't small enough—or affordable enough—to become household staples until the 1970s. Because microwave ovens use electromagnetic radiation rather than fire to heat food, they are generally considered tidier than using a standard oven. But as anyone who's put an uncovered bowl of soup in one of these devices can tell you, microwave cooking can be pretty explosive every now and then. If you are confronting a hard, caked-on mess from microwaved meals past, this is a two-step process. If you're cleaning a recent mess, you can probably skip the first step and go straight to the second.

- First, in a **small bowl** make a paste by mixing **2 tablespoons (30 mL) baking soda** with **1 tablespoon (15 mL) water**. Apply a dab of this mixture to the **scouring side of a damp sponge** and scrub the trouble spots with the paste, reapplying as necessary.

- Next, fill a **medium microwave-safe bowl** about **halfway full of water**. Squeeze the **juice from half a lemon** into the water and add the **leftover rind** before placing the bowl in the microwave. **Heat on high for 5 minutes**, then wipe down the inside of the oven (don't forget the door) with a **damp, lint-free cloth or clean, damp sponge**, rinsing as necessary.

Coffee Maker Cleanse

Coffee makers are, for many of us, the most important appliance in the home. If you run on caffeine, nothing kicks off a new day like a steaming cup of java. Over time, though, all coffee makers begin to suffer from a buildup of residue—coffee is quite oily—that makes coffee taste bitter and unpleasant, no matter how good the beans. Worse, because so many parts of electric coffee makers are never washed (aside from the carafes, which should be washed after every use), they can develop mineral buildup and colonies of bacteria and mold, which could make you sick. **Once every one to two months**, follow this simple procedure to keep your coffee tasting its best.

DRIP COFFEE MAKER

- Remove the **plastic filter basket** from your coffee maker. Over the sink, gently rub down the interior of the basket with the **nonscouring side of a damp sponge**, paying attention to the nooks and crannies between the ribs. Rinse one more time with **warm water** and replace the basket.

- Next, fill the **reservoir** with a mixture of **one-half water** and **one-half white vinegar** and run the coffee maker. When the cycle is complete, empty the vinegar mixture from the carafe, refill the reservoir with water, and run the coffee maker again. Run a third brew cycle with water and dump the water from the carafe. Your maker should be residue-free and ready for the next happy-making batch of brew.

POD COFFEE MAKER

- Fill your sink halfway up with **warm water** and add **1 cup (250 mL) white vinegar**. Remove the **reservoir and its cover, drip tray, and the pod holder** (if removable), and soak in the water-vinegar mixture while you clean the maker.

- Fill a **small bowl** with **¼ cup (60 mL) white vinegar**. Using an **old, soft toothbrush** dipped in the vinegar, scrub the area where the pod holder sits (or the pod holder itself), making sure to remove any coffee residue, grounds, or mineral scale buildup. When the area is clean, wipe it down with a **damp, lint-free cloth**.

- Drain the sink and rub down the coffee maker parts with a **clean, damp sponge**. Reassemble the maker, filling the **reservoir** with a mixture of **one-half white vinegar** and **one-half water**. Place a **large mug** under the spout and run the maker, discarding each cup of vinegar-water that comes out, until the maker tells you the reservoir needs to be filled again. Dump any remaining water-vinegar mixture from the reservoir, refill with plain water, and keep running it until the reservoir needs to be refilled. Repeat this process one more time and your maker should be ready to brew your next cup of joe.

Tea Kettle Cleanse

Whether stovetop or electric, tea kettles are filled exclusively with water—water that is then heated to the boiling point, 212 degrees F (100 degrees C). Common sense suggests that kettles would be the last thing that would need to be cleaned. But water travels through many different environments before it flows through your tap, picking up minerals along the way and, over time, leaving behind trace amounts of those minerals. The most common deposit is calcium carbonate, or limescale, a nontoxic compound that over time can interfere with the taste of the water—and, in the case of electric kettles, with their basic operation. Luckily this deposit is easily tackled with an acid, which breaks it down into carbon dioxide and . . . more water. Depending on how often you use your kettle, you will want to clean it every **one to two months**.

- Fill your **stovetop or electric kettle** halfway with a mixture of **one-half white vinegar** and **one-half water**. Bring the kettle to a **boil**, turn off the heat source, and allow the mixture to sit for **1 hour**.

- Dump the water–vinegar mixture into the sink and, using a **damp, lint-free cloth**, rub away any lingering limescale inside the tea kettle; if the design of your tea kettle makes it difficult to get inside with your hands, push the cloth around the interior with a **wooden spoon**. Rinse the kettle, fill it with **cold water**, and bring the water to a **boil**. Dump the water and repeat one last time.

Tea and Coffee Cup Stain Remover

Tea and coffee make for a delicious and stimulating start to any day or a hard-earned pick-me-up in the afternoon—and for some, a damn-the-torpedoes after-dinner beverage. But both liquids are notorious for leaving stains behind, even in ceramic cups and mugs. To recondition and freshen up your stained cups, follow these instructions.

~~~~~~~~~~

- Add **1 teaspoon (5 mL) baking soda** to the **stained receptacle** and sprinkle just enough **white vinegar** to make a foaming paste in the bottom. Use the **scouring side of a clean, damp sponge** to rub the mild abrasive around the interior of the cup or mug, scrubbing until the stains are gone.

Travel Mug and Water Bottle Cleanse

Travel mugs and stainless-steel water bottles are useful items that also happen to be great for the health of the planet—every time you use one, you avoid purchasing (and throwing away) a one-use plastic item—and the health of your wallet. Here's how to keep these items clean and smelling great.

- The challenge in cleaning **stainless-steel travel mugs** and **water bottles** is that they are often too narrow to fit a sponge inside. To get around this, pour **1 teaspoon (5 mL) baking soda** inside the container and shake it to coat the inside. Add the **juice from 1 lemon wedge** and toss in the **rind**, swirling to combine. Fill the now-foaming vessel to the brim with **boiling water** and let it stand, closing the lid but leaving the drinking spout open, for **15 minutes**. Open the lid and rinse thoroughly with **cold water**.

Drinking Cup and Glass Rim Pretreatment

Lipstick and lip balm marks on the rims of your glasses can be tenacious, surviving even the most efficient dishwasher cycle. Here's how to pretreat your cups and glasses to make sure they come out clean every time.

- Use a **pinch of salt** to scour the rim of the smudged **glass or cup** with your fingers, making sure to go all the way around, inside and out. Place your pretreated glasses in the upper rack of your dishwasher and watch the magic unfold.

Burnt Pot and Pan Cleanse

Perhaps it was a phone call from an old friend, an unexpected knock on the front door, or a call for help from a child in the next room. Whatever the source of the distraction, every cook has left a pot or pan too long over a heat source, transforming what promised to be a great meal into a cleaning catastrophe. Have no fear—even the worst burnt pot or pan can be restored by following these simple steps.

- First, remove as much of the burnt food from the **cookware** as you can.

- Then, depending on the size of the **pot** or **pan**, add **1 to 4 cups (250 mL to 1 L) water** and an **equal amount of white vinegar**. The goal is to cover the bottom of the vessel with **½ to 1 inch (1.25 to 2.5 cm)** of the water-vinegar mixture. Turn the **heat on high** and **boil for 2 minutes**. Remove the pot or pan from the heat and let it cool off for **10 minutes** before discarding the water-vinegar mixture.

- Sprinkle the bottom of the pot or pan with **2 to 3 tablespoons (30 to 45 mL) baking soda**. Using the **scouring side of a clean, damp sponge**, scour the burnt area of the pot or pan until the last traces of the mess are gone. Wash away the baking soda and rinse with **cold water**.

Nonstick Pot and Pan Cleanser

The promise of nonstick cookware is there in its name—nothing is supposed to stick to it, right?—but over time, imperfections in the nonstick coating can develop, lessening its frictionless properties. And every now and then, a sticky, goopy recipe will leave behind a hard-to-clean mess. You should never use steel wool or any other abrasive tool to clean your nonstick cookware because it will scratch the coating—use this simple recipe instead.

- In a **small bowl**, mix together **2 tablespoons (30 mL) lemon juice** and **1 teaspoon (5 mL) baking soda**. Quickly add a couple of teaspoons of this foaming paste to the **non-scouring side of a clean, damp sponge** and rub the **pan** until the mess is cleared away, reapplying the paste as necessary.

Aluminum Pot and Pan Restorer

Aluminum is one of the most popular metals used to make cookware—it's affordable, conducts heat quickly and evenly, and is corrosion-resistant. It also has a warm, attractive luster. But like all metal pots and pans, aluminum cookware can become tarnished by cooked-on food as well as by oxidation (which leaves behind the whitish, powdery substance you sometimes see on the surface). To get your aluminum pots and pans gleaming again, use this cleaning method.

- Squeeze the **juice of half a lemon** into your **pot** or **pan** and fill **halfway with water, reserving the rind**. Place the cookware over **high heat** and **bring to a boil**. Let the lemon water **boil** for **10 minutes** before turning off the heat.

- When the cookware is cool enough to handle, dump the lemon water into the sink and use the **reserved rind** to rub down the parts of the pot or pan that weren't covered by the lemon water, including the outside. Rinse thoroughly with **cold water**.

Cast-Iron Pot and Pan Deep Clean

Cast iron is one of the oldest and most beloved metals used to make cookware, a tradition that extends as far back as sixth-century BCE China. The iron used to manufacture these pots and pans is an alloy made with 2 to 4 percent carbon (as well as other trace materials) in the metal, a mixture that makes it hard enough that it won't warp even when subjected to relatively high temperatures. Like all cookware, cast-iron pans need to be scrubbed and seasoned after every use, but sometimes—especially if they haven't been used in a while—they need extra attention. If your cast iron is covered in stubborn, baked-on grime, stubborn patches of oxidation (rust), burnt food, or if it simply has a sticky coating of old oil and dirt, give it a deep cleaning.

- First, wash the **pan** as well as possible using **a drop or two** of **Castile soap** and the **scouring side of a sponge** you don't mind sacrificing to the cause. Rinse well, then place the pan on the stovetop over **medium heat** until all remaining water has evaporated.

- Pour in **¼ cup (60 mL) grapeseed or other neutral oil** and add **½ cup (125 mL) coarse kosher salt**. When the oil and salt are good and hot, turn off the heat and use a **wad of paper towels held in metal tongs** to scour the inside of the pan with the oily salt, paying special attention to the corners (and being careful not to splash the hot oil over the sides). When the pan is completely cool, discard the salt and wash again in the sink with Castile soap and water. Then season the pan (**Cast-Iron Pot and Pan Seasoning, page 51**) before storing.

Cast-Iron Pot and Pan Seasoning

Cast-iron cookware has many benefits: it's durable; it's among the most affordable options available; it has great heat retention; and, with proper seasoning, it can be almost as nonstick as cookware coated with high-tech materials. Seasoning, which also prevents rusting, polymerizes the oil (transforming it into a tough, slick substance) and bonds it to the surface of the cast iron by the addition of high heat. After cleaning and drying your pans (**Cast-Iron Pot and Pan Deep Clean, page 50**), follow this procedure to season your cookware before you make your next meal.

NOTE: If you use your cast-iron cookware regularly, you only need to season very occasionally—cooking fats on the stovetop achieves the same effect, building up the layers of polymerized oil over time. A properly seasoned pan almost never needs to be cleaned with soap—rinse with **hot water** and reseason after each use instead.

- First, bake your untreated **cast-iron cookware** in the oven at **175 degrees F (80 degrees C)** for **10 minutes** to make sure it is bone dry.

- Remove the pan to the stovetop and turn the oven up to **400 degrees F (205 degrees C)**. While the oven is heating, pour **1 teaspoon (5 mL) grapeseed oil or other neutral oil with a high smoke point** into the pan and use a **paper towel** to wipe the thinnest possible layer of oil all over the surface, inside and out, leaving no excess behind. When the oven is at temperature, place the cookware **upside-down** on the middle rack and bake over a **baking sheet** placed on the bottom rack for **1 hour**. Remove the pan from the oven and allow to cool before using.

NOTE: If you repeat this process one or two more times, you will improve the pan's durable, nonstick coating even more.

Fruit Fly Trap

Common in kitchens around the world, the fruit fly (which is properly called the vinegar fly) is a tiny, mostly harmless, and very irritating pest. They commonly arrive in the home atop produce purchased from the grocery store, where they have an unlimited food supply and lots of mates to choose from. To prevent an infestation from developing in your kitchen—females can lay up to four hundred eggs at a time!—create this trap to lure them to their doom.

- First, place any **soft, ripe (especially overripe) fruit or vegetables** in your refrigerator and thoroughly clean your kitchen sink (especially around the drain).

- Then, in a **small bowl**, gently mix together **1 cup (250 mL) apple cider vinegar**, **a small piece of fruit**, and **2 drops Castile soap**. Cover the opening of the bowl with **aluminum foil** and poke small holes in the foil with a **skewer** or other sharp kitchen implement.

- Attracted to the fruit and vinegar, the flies will find their way inside the holes. Because the flies are so small, they normally take advantage of the surface tension of the vinegar to float—but the Castile soap (a surfactant) disrupts the attraction between the vinegar molecules, meaning any fly that lands on the liquid will slip in and drown.

Sticker Goop Remover

Stickers are everywhere. Commercial food containers, especially glass jars, make good, reusable storage options—but first you need to remove the labels, which are often affixed with a sturdy adhesive meant to withstand the rigors of the grocery store environment. Many household items, from textiles to furniture, are sold with stickers attached. Your car bumper may even be adorned with once-loved-but-now-unwanted stickers. And sometimes, stickers are added to the most unexpected places by creative young minds. To deal with any of these sticky situations, follow these simple guidelines until the residue is gone. You may not need to follow every step, but some combination of them should do the trick.

- After peeling away as much of the sticker as you can by hand, remove the remaining sticker and adhesive residue with a stiff, plastic scraper—a **bowl scraper or expired credit card** works perfectly. If the item is too delicate to scrape, skip to the next step.

- If the object with the sticker can be safely soaked in water, immerse it in a **sink or large bowl** filled with **hot water to cover** for **1 to 2 hours**. This will help soften the sticker and make it easier to remove with a drop or two of **Castile soap** and the **scouring side of a clean, damp sponge**. If the object can't withstand soaking, or if there is still residue remaining, skip to the next step.

- Provided it won't damage the object, apply either **70 percent isopropyl alcohol** (the higher the alcohol percentage, the better) or a **clear spirit** (high-proof vodka is a good choice) to the sticker area with a **clean, lint-free cloth**, rubbing firmly but gently to remove the goop. If you're not sure whether alcohol will damage the object, skip to the next step.

- Soak any remaining sticker residue with **white vinegar** and allow it to sit for **15 minutes** before attempting to wipe away the remaining gunk by hand or with a **damp, lint-free cloth**. If acid will harm the item, skip to the last step.

- As a final step, only to be used on objects that won't be stained or otherwise damaged by this application, rub **olive oil** onto any lingering sticky residue and let it penetrate for a few minutes before scraping away the last of the gunk and cleaning up the oil with **a drop or two** of **Castile soap** applied to a **clean, damp sponge**.

Vegetable Wash

Since many of the vegetables we eat, especially in salads, are raw, it is essential to wash them thoroughly. One of the great gifts of the modern age is increased food production, but this has come at the cost of quality control. As a result of large-scale, industrial farming practices, many potentially harmful (even deadly) pathogens lurk in our produce, including *Cyclospora* (which has been found in raspberries, lettuce, and basil), *E. coli* O157:H7 (a potentially deadly form of an otherwise beneficial bacterium that has been found in many foods, including spinach and other leafy greens), *Listeria* (raw vegetables of several kinds), *Salmonella* (fresh produce of all kinds), and *Shigella* (lettuces, potatoes, onions, parsley). Though this sounds kind of scary, the good news is that all these pathogens are easily cleaned by dousing them in a mild mixture of salt and vinegar, both of which are lethal to most microbes.

- Fill a **large bowl** with **water two-thirds of the way full** and add **1 tablespoon (15 mL) white vinegar** and **¼ teaspoon (1.2 mL) salt**, stirring to combine. Soak your **greens and vegetables** in this solution for **1 minute** before rinsing them under **cold water**. For **root vegetables** like carrots and potatoes, scrub them clean in the salt-vinegar bath with a **dedicated vegetable brush** to remove caked-on dirt before rinsing under **cold water**.

Wilted Greens Reviver

Fresh vegetables should be eaten as close to the moment they are removed from the ground as possible. Our modern-day-a-go-go lifestyle of busy school days, work commutes, and the general hustle-bustle of life makes this impossible, which is where grocery stores and home refrigeration come to the rescue. Greens purchased during your regular shopping trips will keep admirably in the crisper drawer of your refrigerator, but they lose their vibrancy over time. Here's an easy way to resuscitate them.

- In a **very large bowl**, add **1 gallon (4 L) cold water**, an entire **tray of ice cubes**, and **1 tablespoon (15 mL) fine sea salt**. Stir to dissolve as much of the salt as possible before dunking your greens into the water and letting them soak for **15 to 30 minutes**. If you have a large batch of greens in need of revivifying, scale up the water and salt and soak them in your (spotlessly clean!) sink. Either way, wash your greens in a **colander or salad spinner** before serving or cooking.

Kitchen Glove Powder

New dishwashing gloves very helpfully come with a dusting of powder on their interiors to make it a cinch to slip your hands inside. Sadly it takes only one or two plunges into scalding hot water or a vigorous round of sweaty floor mopping for that powder to lose its efficacy.

● A sprinkling of **baking soda** makes an excellent glove powder replacement—shake some into your **dry gloves** before each use to avoid having to peel them off your hands afterward like a brightly colored second skin.

Plastic Storage Container Cleanser

Resealable storage bins are one example of the many uses of plastic, that wonder of modern chemical engineering. One of the downsides of plastic, however, is that it degrades when scratched or exposed to high temperatures, causing it to release any number of chemicals, some of which—phthalates and bisphenol A (BPA), to name two—are not good for people, especially young children. This makes cleaning such containers a tricky proposition. For instance, you should never wash any plastic items in the dishwasher because of its high heat, just as you should never use an abrasive tool like steel wool to scour them. Here's a safe way to clean even the most persistent stains from plastic.

- First, rinse your **plastic containers** clean of any food debris under **warm water**.

- In a **small bowl**, mix together **1 tablespoon (15 mL) lemon juice** or **white vinegar** with **1 tablespoon (15 mL) baking soda**. Add a dab of this foaming paste to the **non-scouring side of a clean, damp sponge** and scrub the plasticware you are cleaning, reapplying the paste as necessary. Allow the scrubbed items to sit for **15 minutes** before rinsing under **cold water**.

Ice Bucket Super Chiller

As any host or hostess knows, an ice bucket is an essential tool for keeping beer, wine, and soft drinks cold during a party. And while preparing an ice bucket seems pretty straightforward—put ice in bucket, put drinks in ice—there is, in fact, a better way. Most importantly, make sure your "bucket" is watertight, whether it's an elegant silver vessel, a galvanized tub, or a jumbo-size plastic garbage can doing double duty as a cooler. Why? Because water plays an important role in a properly prepared ice bucket (and is an unavoidable consequence of melting ice). Here's how to keep your beverages cooler, longer.

- First, fill your **ice bucket with ice** and add **water halfway up** the side of the ice-filled bucket, noting how much water you are adding.

- In a **small bowl**, for every **1 quart (1 L) water** added to the bucket, dissolve **¼ cup (75 g) fine salt** in an **equal amount of hot water**, stirring to dissolve as much as the salt as possible by stirring with a **spoon**. Cool to room temperature and pour this salty sludge into the ice bucket and give the ice water a swirl with a **long-handled wooden spoon**. This trick works to keep your beverages colder because the salt lowers the freezing point of the water, making it possible for the ice to supercool the water surrounding your drinks.

CHAPTER 3

THE LIVING ROOM

The living room is so called because so much of life happens within its walls. It is the room where we have parties, watch movies, play games, and generally spend a lot of time in each other's company. And when you're alone, well, it's where you sack out on the couch and read a book or binge-watch your favorite show. All of which is to say, it gets a fair amount of daily use. The recipes in this chapter will help you keep the room looking (and smelling!) its very best.

Rug and Carpet Shampoo

While delightful to walk across in bare feet and surprisingly effective as soundproofing, rugs and carpets are also—how do I put this delicately?—filth magnets. Whether an area rug or wall-to-wall carpeting, these decorative floor coverings collect skin flakes, hair, tracked-in dirt, crumbs, and who-knows-what-else. Regular vacuuming can handle most of this, but every now and then your rugs and carpets will need a proper shampoo. Your feet will thank you.

NOTE: This works for both synthetic and natural fibers, but you may want to test-clean a small section of rug before tackling a larger area.

- Begin by thoroughly **vacuuming** the **rug or carpet**.

- In a **large mixing bowl**, combine **¼ cup (60 mL) liquid Castile soap**, **¼ cup (60 mL) water**, **2 tablespoons (30 mL) baking soda**, and **10 drops essential oil of your choice**. Using a **hand mixer or whisk** (this option will be a bit of a workout), beat the mixture until it forms a stiff foam. Spread this foam mixture as evenly as possible over the rug or carpet you are cleaning and gently scrub using a **large, lightly damp sponge or sponge mop**. Allow the rug or carpet to air dry, then vacuum again.

Rug and Carpet Brightener

Carpets and rugs are the hardest-working textiles in the home. In fact they are so taken for granted that they're the basis of a popular saying about thoughtless mistreatment: to "walk all over someone" like a rug is to trample on them as if they barely exist. Because of the daily abuse they receive, rugs and carpets fade over time. But if you take the time to acknowledge their heroic service **every two to three months** by applying this simple treatment, you'll be amazed at how their color can be revived and sustained.

- In a **medium bowl**, mix **½ cup (125 mL) white vinegar, 1 cup (250 mL) salt**, and **2 cups (500 mL) hot water** until thoroughly combined. Using a **large, damp sponge**, apply this mixture in a circular motion to the entire surface of the **rug or carpet**, being careful to get the fibers damp but not to soak through to the backing. Continue to apply until you've treated the entire surface.

- Finally, using a **box or oscillating fan**, dry the rug thoroughly. This process can take from **6 to 24 hours**, depending on the depth of the pile.

NOTE: This amount of liquid is enough for roughly **10 square feet (1 square meter)**; scale up the quantity as needed.

Rug and Carpet Deodorizer

Once again, it's odor-absorbent baking soda to the rescue! Just keep in mind that this treatment is for regular odor control. If, say, your pets have done something unthinkable on your carpet or rug, stop reading immediately and head straight to **Rug and Carpet Stain Cleaner (page 65)**. Depending on how much use your rug or carpet gets, you will want to follow this simple deodorizing procedure **every four to eight weeks** to keep them from smelling like a sweaty teenager.

NOTE: This procedure works just as well on upholstered furniture.

- Begin by **vacuuming** the **rug or carpet** you want to deodorize.

- Then, using a **flour sifter or fine-mesh stainless-steel strainer**, sprinkle **1 cup (250 mL) baking soda** (or more, depending on the size of the rug or carpet) across the area. Allow the baking soda to sit on the rug for a **minimum of 3 hours**, though **overnight is best**—just make sure to limit human and animal traffic during this period. Finally, vacuum up the baking soda.

Rug and Carpet Stain Cleaner

Floor coverings have many wonderful qualities, from sound dampening to providing comfort for your feet, but they have some drawbacks too. When you (or your pets) spill something on them, for example, it's important to spring into action right away or else risk permanent damage. Here are quick and effective cleaning solutions for rug and carpet stains (as well as fabric furniture upholstery stains) of all kinds.

OILY STAINS

- If you spill or drop something oily onto your **rug or carpet**, start by immediately picking up any solids, being careful not to grind any into the carpet pile. Blot any excess with a **damp rag or paper towel**, in an upward, plucking motion. Sprinkle **baking soda, 1 tablespoon (15 mL) at a time**, onto the slightly damp stain in a small mound to cover. Let dry for **at least 3 hours, but preferably overnight.**

- **Vacuum** up the dried baking soda and clean any caked-on baking soda with a **damp rag or paper towel**. If the stain persists, use a **clean, damp sponge** to dab at the stain, then repeat the above process a second time.

→

NON-OILY STAINS

- Non-oily substances are easier to clean but need to be addressed just as quickly to minimize staining. First, blot away any residue from the spill with a **damp rag or paper towel** in an upward, plucking motion. In a **small bowl**, mix together **2 tablespoons (30 mL) baking soda** with **1 tablespoon (15 mL) water**; if you are wrestling with a larger spill, scale up the quantity as necessary using the same 2:1 ratio of ingredients. Apply this paste in a thick mound to the spill area and let dry for **at least 3 hours, but preferably overnight**.

- **Vacuum** up the dried baking soda, then clean any remaining powder with a **clean, damp sponge**. If the stain persists, repeat. If the stain won't come up, it might be time to call in a pro.

Multipurpose Floor Cleaner

Around the mid-twentieth century, waxing became the go-to method for maintaining a beautiful glow underfoot. Since then, many flooring options have come along that require far less maintenance. If you aren't sure what type of floor you have, the solution here is safe for use on many types, including solid wood, engineered hardwood (a layer of hardwood bonded to plywood), laminate wood floors (particleboard covered with a thin photo laminate), bamboo, modern no-wax vinyl, urethane, and glazed ceramic. To clean natural, unglazed stone floors (including terra-cotta), see **Natural Stone Floor Cleaner (page 68)**.

- First, **sweep or vacuum** the **floor** you plan to clean.

- Then, in a **large bucket** mix **1 gallon (4 L) warm water**, **2 cups (500 mL) white vinegar**, and **10 to 20 drops essential oil of your choice**. Using a **nonabrasive sponge mop**, apply a light coat of the mixture, cleaning the mop head after every few strokes, until the entire floor is clean. Use a **dry mop** to soak up any remaining moisture.

Natural Stone Floor Cleaner

Natural stone is a popular flooring choice because it is both durable and attractive—it is also quite porous, which means it retains dirt and grime. And because acids (such as lemon juice and vinegar) as well as bases (such as baking soda or Castile soap) can damage the surface of natural stone, it is important to use a neutral-pH solution when cleaning these beautiful floors.

- First, **sweep or vacuum** the **floor** you plan to clean.

- In a **large bucket**, mix **1 gallon (4 L) warm water**, **1 cup (250 mL) 70 percent isopropyl alcohol**, and **10 to 20 drops essential oil of your choice**. Using a **nonabrasive sponge mop**, apply a light coat of the mixture to the **floor**, cleaning the mop head after every few strokes, until the entire surface is clean. Use a **dry mop** to soak up any remaining moisture.

Wood Floor Polish

In an ideal world, your beautiful solid wood floors would get a rewaxing every six months to one year. But waxing is a big, complicated process that can render huge stretches of your home off-limits as the wax dries. Luckily this recipe makes an excellent substitute for a full-blown wax treatment—use it **every month or so** and your wood floors will retain their warm glow for far longer.

- In a **large bucket**, mix **1 gallon (4 L) water, ¾ cup (180 mL) olive oil**, and **10 to 20 drops essential oil of your choice**. Using a **nonabrasive sponge mop**, apply a light coat of this mixture to the **floor**, dipping the mop head after every few strokes, until the entire surface is shining. Use a **dry mop or clean, lint-free cloth** to buff the floor to a high shine.

All-Purpose Glass Cleaner

Whether you're looking into your own reflection in a mirror, at a favorite work of art, through a window, or at a photo of your beloved Aunt Bethune, you want the glass protecting the object of your gaze to be as clean as possible. To remove fingerprints, streaks, and other blemishes from glass, use this multipurpose formula.

- In a **clean 16-ounce (500 mL) glass spray bottle**, mix together **1 cup (250 mL) distilled water**, **½ cup (125 mL) 70 percent isopropyl alcohol**, and **3 tablespoons (45 mL) white vinegar**. Replace the spray nozzle, and the cleaner is ready to go.

NOTE: When wiping up this (or any) glass cleaner, make sure to use a **clean, lint-free cloth or microfiber towel**—paper towels and many other types of fabric will leave behind fibers.

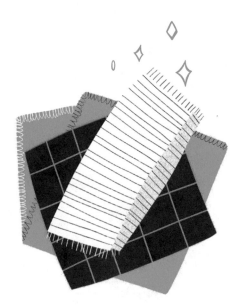

Window Anti-Freeze

If you live in a cold climate, you have no doubt experienced frost buildup on your windows during a deep freeze. This is caused by water condensing on the windowpanes, then freezing. If you have a cold front approaching, it is a simple matter to Jack Frost–proof your windows with this recipe, which takes advantage of the fact that the addition of salt lowers the freezing point of water (though if you live somewhere that regularly gets subzero weather, this trick will be a little less effective).

NOTE: This recipe also works on **car windows**, though be extra careful to wipe away any brine that gets on the rubber gaskets.

● In a **clean 16-ounce (500 mL) glass spray bottle**, mix together **1 tablespoon (15 mL) salt** with **2 cups (500 mL) warm water**, reattach the nozzle, and shake until the salt has dissolved. Spray this on your **windows**, inside and out, and **thoroughly dry with a clean, lint-free cloth** to prevent frost buildup.

Vacuum Bag Deodorizer

Here's a familiar scenario: you're running the vacuum around the living room, picking up dirt and pet hair, maybe some crumbs, and you begin to notice a funky odor—a little moldy, maybe even a little like burning rubber. Hard to believe, but it's actually your vacuum cleaner stinking up the place. Sometimes just changing the bag or emptying the tank isn't enough to combat these bad smells— luckily, there's a more reliable solution.

- Discard the full bag from your **vacuum cleaner**; if your cleaner has a reusable tank instead, empty it, spray it with **All-Purpose Cleanser (page 18)**, and wipe it dry with a paper towel.

- In a **small bowl**, combine **2 tablespoons (30 mL) baking soda** with **10 to 15 drops essential oil of your choice (lemon or lavender** are both excellent for this purpose). Sprinkle the scented baking soda into the **new bag** or into the **tank** before reassembling the vacuum. If you do this every time you change the bag or tank, your vacuum will deodorize your entire home every time you use it.

Water-Glass Ring Remover

Wood is one of the oldest building materials in the world, with whole empires (including the Roman Empire) built thanks to the long-distance timber trade. Today a globe-spanning trade network provides access to wood furniture made from a wide variety of trees from around the world. For all its warmth and natural beauty, however, wood (even hardwood) can show signs of wear and tear rather easily. In particular, condensation from drinking glasses can leave behind unsightly white rings, a result of moisture getting into the layers of protective varnish. To erase these marks, follow this quick procedure.

NOTE: If the water stains are dark, it could mean the water has stained the wood beneath the layers of veneer; if this is the case, the surface may need to be refinished.

- In a **small bowl** mix together **2 tablespoons (30 mL) baking soda** and **1 tablespoon (15 mL) water**. Using a **clean, lint-free cloth**, gently rub this absorbent paste around the **ring**, in the direction of the wood grain wherever possible. After wiping up the paste, rub a few drops of **grapeseed or olive oil** into the surface and buff with a **paper towel or clean, lint-free cloth** to restore its luster.

TV and Computer Monitor Cleaner

Because many TV and computer monitor screens are made of plastic, keep vinegar and other acids away from them—this means you shouldn't, for instance, use the **All-Purpose Glass Cleaner (page 70)**. Fortunately the formula for making a highly effective screen cleaner is simple—and just as effective as (and much less expensive than) any commercial product.

* In a **clean 4-ounce (125 mL) glass spray bottle**, add ¼ cup **(60 mL) 70 percent isopropyl alcohol** and ¼ cup (60 mL) distilled **water**. Replace the spray nozzle, shake well, and your screen cleaner is ready to use.

NOTE: Use a **clean, lint-free cloth** to wipe up this spray—paper towels and many fabrics will leave behind fibers.

Painted-Wall Cleaner

Walls are the unsung heroes of every room, holding up the ceiling as well as the occasional unsteady houseguest. Not surprisingly, they get quite dirty—you and your pets brush up against them, your housemates leave fingerprints and handprints all over the place, and objects are constantly banging into them. Kitchen walls, in particular, get very grimy because cooking kicks up airborne grease and other particulates. The invention of the "magic sponge" (which is made of cured melamine resin, an ultrafine abrasive) has gone a long way toward making the erasure of unsightly marks on walls a snap, but not for overall grime. Next time you notice your walls looking a little grubby, use this method to clean them.

- If your **walls** are visibly dusty or covered in cobwebs, begin by dusting with a **clean, lint-free cloth or microfiber brush attached to a pole** or using a **cordless vacuum fitted with the dust brush** (which has the softest fibers and won't scratch the paint).

- In a **large bucket**, mix together **2 quarts (2 L) water** with **½ cup (125 mL) white vinegar** (for any oil-based, semi-gloss, or glossy painted surfaces) or **½ cup (125 mL) Castile soap** (for latex, matte, satin, or eggshell paints). Dip the head of a **clean, long-handled sponge mop or a clean, nonabrasive sponge** into this mixture and squeeze out as much moisture as possible before cleaning the walls. Work top to bottom, wringing out the mop or sponge periodically. Dry immediately with a **clean, lint-free cloth**.

Wallpaper Cleaner

The earliest use of decorative paper to cover the walls of the home seems to be sometime in the second century BCE in China. By the sixteenth century CE, wallpaper had become quite popular among Europe's booming merchant class. At that time, wallpaper was handmade in individual squares using block-printing techniques, but the innovations of the Industrial Revolution eventually led to new methods of production that made wallpaper cheaper and widely available. It also led to the invention of different kinds of wallpaper, as reflected in the wide range you can find today, including cellulose (traditional paper), fabric, vinyl, fiberglass, bamboo, and flocked. Before cleaning your wallpaper, make sure you know which kind you have—they can't all be cleaned the same way. If you're unsure what kind it is, test any cleaning method on a small, out-of-the-way area before tackling the whole wall.

- All **wallpapers** can be cleaned by dusting with a **clean, lint-free cloth or microfiber brush attached to a pole** or using a **cordless vacuum fitted with the dust brush** (which has the softest fibers and won't scratch the paper). Use long, straight strokes starting at the top and moving downward. If you have any type of **unflocked wallpaper**, the British historic preservation society English Heritage also recommends the nineteenth-century practice of lightly brushing away dirt and dust with **slices of fresh bread**.

- If your wallpaper is made of **vinyl** or **fiberglass**, you may follow the **dusting or vacuuming** with a light wash. In a **large bowl**, mix **1 gallon (4 L) water** with **1 quart (1 L) white vinegar** or **¼ cup (60 mL) Castile soap**. Dip the head of a **clean, long-handled sponge mop or a clean, nonabrasive sponge** into this mixture and squeeze out as much moisture as possible before cleaning the wallpaper. Work top to bottom with light strokes. Dry immediately with a **clean, lint-free cloth**.

NOTE: Because wallpaper attracts a lot of dirt and dust in its fibers, try to clean it **once or twice per month** to prevent permanent staining.

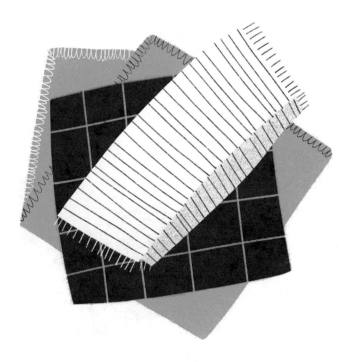

Wall Stain Remover

In a universe where objects collide, walls get stained—dusty grease patches, crayon drawings, and rubber scuff marks are all evidence of this fundamental truth. If you have wall space that has taken a hit and can't be cleaned using the **Painted-Wall Cleaner (page 75)** alone, try this gentle abrasive on your painted walls (and your vinyl and fiberglass wallpaper) to remove stubborn stains.

- In a **medium bowl**, make a paste of **½ cup (125 mL) baking soda** and **¼ cup (60 mL) water**. Add a dab of this paste to the **non-scouring side of a clean, damp sponge** and scrub the stain, reapplying the paste as necessary. When the stain is gone, rinse the sponge with clean water, wring it out, and wipe the area clean. Dry immediately with a **clean, lint-free cloth**.

Light-Duty Spackle

One time-honored way to keep common areas (and relationships) fresh is to change things up every now and then. Moving the furniture around can create a whole new feel in a living space, for instance, and so can changing up the placement of photos and artwork on the walls. Sadly, when a shift like this happens, you will discover unsightly nail holes and dings in the walls. To fill them in, use this simple spackle.

- Add **1 tablespoon (15 mL) salt** and **2 tablespoons (30 mL) boiling water** to a **small bowl** and stir with a **fork** until the salt has dissolved. Allow the mixture to cool for **2 minutes**, then add **2 tablespoons (30 mL) cornstarch**, **2 tablespoons (30 mL) white flour**, and **1 teaspoon (5 mL) baking soda**, and stir until a thick putty has formed. Apply the spackle to the hole using a **putty knife or steel spatula**. Allow to dry for **24 hours** before sanding and applying paint. Store leftover spackle in a **clean, resealable 4-ounce (120 mL) glass jar**.

Ceiling Fan Cleanse

You'd think that the rapid movement of a ceiling fan blade would prevent it from being covered in dirt and dust, but the opposite is true: its oscillating motion actually causes the blades to pick up *far more* of the airborne grime in your home. Here's how to get those furry fan blades clean.

- First, grab a ladder. Spray each **blade**, top and bottom, with **All-Purpose Cleanser (page 18)**. Slip an **old pillowcase** or **T-shirt** over the fan blade, gently closing it around the base of the blade and carefully drawing the fabric toward yourself to trap the dust inside. Proceed one fan blade at a time, rotating the fan until you've cleaned them all. Lightly spray the blades one more time and wipe up any remaining dirt with the outside of the pillowcase or shirt.

Air Conditioner Filter Cleanse

The removable filter in your air conditioner becomes clogged with dust, pollen, and other airborne materials faster than you might think. When this happens, the air conditioner stops working as efficiently, which causes it to use more electricity and eventually to recirculate those contaminants in your home. Clean the filter **once per month** during warm months to keep your air conditioner performing at its peak.

• Fill your **kitchen sink or another container that can hold the filters lying flat) 4 inches (11 cm) full** with **2 parts warm water** and **1 part white vinegar**. One by one, dip your **filters**, dusty side down, into this mixture and gently agitate them for a few seconds before setting them aside on your kitchen counter. When every filter has been soaked, drain the sink and, using the sprayer, rinse the filters under **cold water** to remove any remaining dust and dirt. Lay the filters out to dry in the sun, if you can, or on a towel before putting them back into your air conditioners.

Air Freshener and Deodorizing Spray

There are many reasons to add a scent to your home, whether to set a holiday mood or to mask the fallout from your puppy's recent misadventure on the living room carpet. Whatever the reason, here are two ways to introduce a new, more welcome odor to any situation. And for the record, I highly recommend keeping a bottle of homemade deodorizing spray next to the reading material in your bathroom (right next to the **Toilet Bowl Deodorizer, page 125**).

~~~~~~~~~

AIR FRESHENER

- In a **small, decorative bowl or dish**, mix **2 tablespoons (30 mL) baking soda** and **20 to 25 drops of essential oil of your choice**, stirring as you add the essential oil. Once these ingredients are fully incorporated, set the bowl or dish in an out-of-the-way location where kids and pets can't get to it.

DEODORIZING SPRAY

- Add **¼ cup (60 mL) 70 percent isopropyl alcohol, 20 to 25 drops of essential oil of your choice**, and water to fill to a **clean 16-ounce (500 mL) glass spray bottle**. Replace the spray nozzle, shake well, and your take-it-anywhere air-freshening spray is ready for action.

Wicker Furniture Reconditioner

Wicker and rattan furniture have a lovely, retro vibe that introduce a natural element into your home decor in an elegant way. And while cleaning and reconditioning wicker might seem like a challenge, it's actually quite simple.

- First, remove any textiles or cushions from the **wicker furniture**.

- In a **wide, shallow bowl**, mix ¼ cup **(75 g) salt** and **1 cup (250 mL) warm water**, stirring to completely dissolve the salt. Dip a **stiff brush** into the mixture, shake off any excess, and scrub the wicker surface, reapplying the salty water every few strokes but being careful not to soak the wicker. If possible, completely dry the furniture in the sun or use a **box or oscillating fan** before replacing the fabric or cushions.

Lemon-Scented Wood Furniture Cleanser

Feather dusters are a timeless symbol of house cleaning, but it turns out that bird feathers are not that good at attracting dust—they tend to just move the dust around. A much better option is the microfiber cloth, which is a little less absorbent when it comes to liquids than cotton cloth but an absolute dust magnet. Skip the feathers and go for the microfiber when you use this recipe to clean your wood furniture.

In a **clean 16-ounce (500 mL) glass spray bottle**, mix **1 cup (250 mL) white vinegar**, **½ teaspoon (2.5 mL) olive oil**, and **5 to 10 drops lemon essential oil**. Replace the spray nozzle and shake well before every use. Use a **microfiber cloth** to wipe up the spray and any trapped dust and dirt. If the furniture you are cleaning is a **mix of wood and upholstery**, spray directly onto the microfiber cloth before cleaning the wood—this will prevent any oil in the spray from staining the fabric.

Lemon-Scented Wood Furniture Polish

When I was a kid, I knew it was going to be a serious day of cleaning when a certain brand of furniture polish, in its trademark yellow-and-brown spray can, made its appearance. It meant that all the exposed wood on the living room furniture and the dining table were about to be buffed and the apartment was going to smell like lemons. Now, though, it is recommended *not* to use any silicone-based commercial polishes like the old yellow-and-brown. They leave behind a gunky residue that over time dulls the shine, attracts more dust, and complicates any future refinishing. Use this simple, all-natural preparation instead.

- Begin by dusting and cleaning your **wood furniture**, using the **Lemon-Scented Wood Furniture Cleanser (page 84)**.

- In a **clean 16-ounce (500 mL) glass spray bottle**, mix **1 cup (250 mL) olive oil**, **2 tablespoons (30 mL) white vinegar**, and **5 drops lemon essential oil**. Replace the nozzle and shake well before every use. Spray a small amount directly onto **all-wood furniture** and buff to a shine with a **clean, lint-free cloth**. If the furniture is a **mix of wood and upholstery**, spray directly onto the lint-free cloth before rubbing into the wood—this will prevent any oil from staining the fabric.

NOTE: You can substitute **lemon juice** for vinegar in this recipe, but make sure it is strained free of any pulp.

Upholstered Furniture Deodorizer

In the best of all worlds, children would be clean and tidy, pets would remain on the floor, and nobody would eat a meal while sitting on the couch. Sadly, however, we live in the real world, where bad smells happen to good furniture. Here's how to bring a small bit of order to an otherwise chaotic universe.

- Begin by **vacuuming** your **furniture**, using the brush attachment to get into the corners.

- Then, using a **flour sifter or fine-mesh stainless-steel strainer**, sprinkle **½ cup (125 mL) baking soda** (or more, depending on the size of the furniture) across the affected area. Allow the baking soda to remain on the furniture for a **minimum of 3 hours**, though **overnight is best**. And for the love of jellybeans, keep the pets, children, and Uncle Miltie off the settee while the baking soda is doing its thing. Finally, vacuum up the baking soda.

Upholstered Furniture Cleaner

Upholstery is kind of like a super low-pile rug for your furniture, a skin made of fabric, there to protect the contents from the rigors of its environment. It's up to you to keep your furniture's skin clean, a process that should happen **every 1 to 2 months**, depending on how heavily the furniture is used.

- In a **clean 16-ounce (500 mL) glass spray bottle**, mix **1 cup (250 mL) water**, **2 tablespoons (30 mL) Castile soap**, **1 tablespoon (15 mL) white vinegar**, and **½ teaspoon (2.5 mL) baking soda**. Replace the spray nozzle and shake gently to combine. To use, spray all over the surface of your **upholstered furniture**, gently scrubbing with a **clean, damp, nonabrasive sponge**. Blot dry with a **clean, lint-free cloth**.

Upholstered Furniture Stain Remover

If your wingback reading chair, Chesterfield sofa, or tufted chaise longue has been on the receiving end of a spill that left a stain, follow these steps to minimize the damage (though not on silk).

- In a **small bowl**, mix **½ cup (125 mL) baking soda** and **¼ cup (60 mL) water** to make a thick paste. Rub the paste into the stained **upholstery** with your fingers, covering the affected area in a thick layer. Allow the paste to dry, around **3 hours**, then brush off with a **stiff brush or dry sponge**. **Vacuum** thoroughly to remove the last remnants of dried baking soda; if some baking soda remains caked on, use a **clean, damp sponge** to remove the rest and blot dry with a **clean, lint-free cloth**.

Leather Furniture Cleaner

Flexible and strong, leather is used to make all sorts of everyday items, from belts and shoes to coats and household tools. And furniture, of course. If treated properly, leather furniture is quite durable and acquires a lovely patina of wear over time. Mistreat it, however, and the material can become quite shabby—discolored and covered in scratches and cracks. Clean it like this and your furniture will look its best for much longer, especially when followed with the **Leather Furniture Conditioner (page 90)**.

NOTE: This can also be used to clean leather clothing, from coats to pants.

~~~~~~~~~~

• Begin by **vacuuming** your **leather furniture** with the brush attachment, getting into all the nooks and crannies.

• In a **clean 16-ounce (500 mL) glass spray bottle**, mix **1 cup (250 mL) olive oil**, **½ cup (125 mL) white vinegar**, and **5 drops lemon or orange essential oil**. Replace the spray nozzle and shake well before every use. Spray the furniture all over, then buff the leather, using circular motions, with a **clean, lint-free cloth**.

Leather Furniture Conditioner

After you've given your favorite couch or club chair a thorough cleaning with the **Leather Furniture Cleaner (page 89)**, make sure to condition the surface using this simple treatment to keep it supple and protect it against the wear-and-tear of daily use.

NOTE: If you clean and condition your leather furniture (and clothing), it will last longer and resist stains.

● Dip the corner of a **clean, lint-free cloth** into a jar of **coconut oil** and rub the surface of the **furniture**, using circular motions and reapplying the coconut oil as necessary. When the entire surface has been covered, **let stand for 30 minutes**. Use **another clean, lint-free cloth** to buff the entire piece of furniture, making sure to wipe up any leftover oil.

Leather Furniture Stain Remover

Every now and then life will deal a blow to your favorite leather loveseat or sectional (or floor-length leather duster) in the form of a stain. When accidents happen, the best thing you can do is spring into action immediately, first by trying to clean the area with a **clean, damp, lint-free cloth**. If that doesn't work, here is how to treat common types of spills.

NOTE: The lighter the color of the leather, the more careful you should be when cleaning stains—stop regularly to let the treatment dry and check if the stain is responding; if not, consider calling in a pro.

INK STAINS AND SHOE POLISH

- Dip a **cotton ball or cotton swab** into **50 percent isopropyl alcohol** and rub at the stain to erase it from the surface of the **leather**. Allow the area to dry completely to see if the stain is gone. Recondition afterward with a dab of **coconut oil** rubbed into the area of the stain with a **clean, lint-free cloth**.

OTHER STAINS

- Most other stains (red wine, grease, and so on) can be cleaned like this. In a **small bowl**, mix **2 tablespoons (30 mL) lemon juice** with **2 tablespoons (30 mL) baking soda**. Dip the corner of a **clean, lint-free cloth** into the foaming mixture and rub out the stain, reapplying as necessary. Allow the area to dry completely to see if the stain is gone. Recondition afterward with a dab of **coconut oil** rubbed into the area of the stain with a **clean, lint-free cloth**.

Leather Scratch Eraser

Durable as it is, leather does scratch easily, but you can touch up minor abrasions with this easy technique.

- In a **small bowl**, mix **1 teaspoon (5 mL) olive oil** and **1 teaspoon (5 mL) lemon or orange essential oil**. Dip a **cotton ball or cotton swab** into the mixture and rub it into the scratch.

Hinge Lubricant

The squeaky hinge is a trademark sound of the haunted house because it suggests that the house was abandoned long, long ago. The truth is, squeaks also happen in non-haunted houses—over time, hinges accumulate dirt and dust that increase the friction within the moving parts, and that friction is the source of the screechy sound. If you'd like the doors in your home to operate smoothly and without any suggestion of the supernatural, try this.

- Using the **All-Purpose Cleanser (page 18)**, spray the **hinges** on the creaky door and wipe them down with a **clean, lint-free cloth**. Fill a **2-ounce (60 mL) dropper bottle** with **olive oil**. Starting at the top, under the top of the hinge pin (the rod that holds the hinge together), and moving downward, use the dropper to squeeze a drop or two of olive oil into the cracks between each section of the hinge. After finishing each hinge, swing the door back and forth to distribute the oil within the hinge before moving on to the next.

- When all the hinges have been oiled, swing the door back and forth once more, listening for any further sounds. Keep applying the oil to the squeaky hinge until the door swings silently. Clean any oil drips up immediately with a **paper towel or lint-free cloth**.

Smoke Odor Remediation

Whether from a burnt meal, a nearby house fire, or wildfires, smoke leaves behind a tenacious and unpleasant odor. Getting rid of it is a multistep process that puts several of the other procedures in this book to good use. Weather permitting, **open any windows—**circulating fresh air through the smoky room you are trying to deodorize is the best way to begin the process.

- Clean any **textiles** (curtains, drapes, furniture coverings, and so on) in the room—fabric is an odor magnet. Wash all textiles that are laundry-safe in the **washing machine** with **Laundry Deodorizer (page 135)**. Any fabrics that can't be washed should be laid flat (outdoors, ideally, but at the very least in a room that doesn't smell like smoke), **vacuumed**, and sprinkled on both sides with a generous coating of **baking soda**. Allow the baking soda to absorb the odors for **12 to 24 hours** before vacuuming up the baking soda.

- If there are **rugs or carpeting** in the room, follow the instructions for **Rug and Carpet Shampoo (see page 62)** and then **Rug and Carpet Deodorizer (see page 64)**, allowing the **baking soda** to absorb odors for **12 to 24 hours** before vacuuming. This also goes for any **upholstered furniture**.

- Any **wood, metal, or glass furniture** will have to be cleaned too. Treat any hard surfaces (except for natural stone) with **All-Purpose Cleanser (page 18)** and the **windows** with **All-Purpose Glass Cleaner (page 70)**. To clean any **natural stone surfaces**, use **Natural Stone Countertop Cleanser (page 25)**.

- Smoke is made up of a Pandora's box of microparticles that settle everywhere, including on the walls and ceiling. Follow the instructions for **Painted Wall Cleaner (see page 75)** or **Wallpaper Cleaner (see page 76)**, depending on what kind of **walls** you have, paying special attention to the **ceiling**. If the fire was in the kitchen, wash the **cabinets** with **All-Purpose Cleanser (page 18)**.

- If you have **air purifiers** or **air conditioners** in the room, their **filters** will need to be cleaned or replaced. Follow the instructions for **Air Conditioner Filter Cleanse (see page 81)** or consult the air purifier instructions for cleaning the carbon filter or replacing the HEPA filter.

- Finally, set a few **small bowls** half-filled with **baking soda** around the room and leave them there for **at least 48 hours**, giving them time to absorb any lingering odors. By the end of this process, the smoky smell should be much improved. If you want to add a new odor to mask any lingering traces of the smoke, follow the instructions for **Air Freshener and Deodorizing Spray (see page 82)**.

CHAPTER 4

THE BEDROOM

Chances are that you, like nearly every other human being on the planet, will spend a full third of your life in the land of nod. Since most of those sleeping hours will be spent in your bedroom, it means you will spend more time in that one room than in any other in the home—especially when you factor in all the lounging, reading, getting dressed and undressed, physically expressing your fondest feelings for your partner (or partners) or yourself, and avoiding family members during their semiannual visits. The recipes in this chapter will help you preserve your bedroom as the sweet-smelling, sparkling clean, and inviting sanctuary it was meant to be.

Pillow Deodorizer

Most animals, including humans, like to sleep with their heads resting on *something*, even if that something is just another part of their bodies (a forelimb, for instance). It shouldn't come as a surprise, then, that the earliest record of pillow use is ancient, dating back to 7000 BCE Mesopotamia, when the wealthy slept with their heads supported by wooden or stone supports that looked a lot like oversize oarlocks. Today's pillows are mercifully made of soft fabrics, memory foam, cooling gel, and other miracles of modern manufacturing, but one of their disadvantages is that they get smelly—our heads sweat a lot, for one thing, and our breath doesn't exactly improve as we sleep. Pillows should be washed **every four to six months**, but in the meantime, they should be **deodorized once per month**.

- Remove the pillowcase from the **pillow** and sprinkle ¼ **cup (60 mL) baking soda** on both sides of the pillow. Allow the baking soda to sit for **at least 1 hour** before **vacuuming** it up. For an extra bit of odor control (and if you don't mind your pillow smelling lemon-fresh for a day or two), spray the pillow with **All-Purpose Cleanser (page 18)** and immediately wipe down the pillow with a **clean, damp sponge**. Air-dry (**in sunlight, if possible**) before putting on a new pillowcase.

NOTE: If you'd prefer a different scent, add **5 drops essential oil of your choice** (lavender is said to promote restfulness) to the baking soda before sprinkling, and use a **plain, full-strength vinegar spray** instead of the All-Purpose Cleanser.

Mattress Deodorizer

Like pillows, mattresses provide a world of comfort to us in our most vulnerable hours, but in this service they absorb some less-than-savory, odor-causing substances: sweat, dirt, skin flakes, dust mites, hair, dander, and . . . well, other stuff. One way to combat the funky smells that can develop in our mattresses is to deodorize them using this procedure **every two to four months**.

- After stripping the bed of all its linens, including any bed pads, **vacuum** the **mattress** thoroughly using the **upholstery brush attachment**. In a **small bowl**, add **15 to 20 drops essential oil of your choice** (I recommend **eucalyptus or rosemary**) to **1 cup (250 mL) baking soda**, tossing to combine. Using a **flour sifter or fine-mesh stainless-steel strainer**, sprinkle scented baking soda across the area. Allow the baking soda to sit on the mattress for **1 to 3 hours** before vacuuming again.

NOTE: If you prefer an unscented experience, leave the essential oil out of the mix.

Mattress Stain Removal

Without going into too many details, it should be acknowledged that mattresses get stained with all sorts of fluids, ranging from the innocuous (water) to the deeply unpleasant (vomit). To prevent the sights and smells of such stains from becoming permanent features of your mattress, **it is important to address them immediately**.

- Strip the **bed** of all its linens, including any bed pads, and pretreat them with one of the **Stain Pretreatments (page 132)** before putting them into the **washing machine**.

- If the mattress is still wet, blot away as much of the fluid as possible using **paper towels or a clean, lint-free cloth**. In a **small bowl**, make a paste of **½ cup (125 mL) warm (not hot) water**, **¼ cup (60 mL) baking soda**, and **1 tablespoon (15 mL) fine salt**. Gently rub the paste into the stain and allow it to dry, **around 1 hour**. **Vacuum** the dried paste using the **upholstery brush attachment**.

- Using the **All-Purpose Cleanser (page 18)**, spray the affected area and pat dry with **paper towels or a clean, lint-free cloth**. Allow the mattress to completely dry before replacing the bed linens.

Lube

For intimate moments spent alone or with a partner (or partners), nothing elevates the experience like a good lubricant. There are several characteristics of a quality lube, including friction reduction (known as lubricity) and high viscosity (which makes it last longer). And, last but not least, a lube should be safe to put on our skin and inside our body cavities, and to ingest. With these qualities in mind, and after extensive research, here are two natural formulas that avoid silicone, propylene glycol, and other ingredients commonly found in commercial lubes that can cause allergic reactions and other complications.

~~~~~~~~

WATER-BASED

- If you are using condoms, dental dams, or other latex-based devices, you might want to use a water-based lubricant—in clinical studies, oil-based lubricants have been shown to weaken latex.

- In a **small pot**, combine **1 cup (250 mL) water** and **4 teaspoons (20 mL) cornstarch** and bring to a **boil**, stirring until the cornstarch has dissolved. Cool to room temperature and pour this mixture into a **clean 8-ounce (250 mL) squeeze bottle**. Apply (and reapply) as necessary.

OIL-BASED

- If latex-based devices and allergies are not an issue, the following three words describe what is, without question, the slickest, longest-lasting, and most delicious lube you will ever use: **virgin coconut oil**. Apply liberally (and make sure to protect your bed linens and upholstered furniture with a towel).

Closet Freshener

The clothes closet is the archive of our daily attire—from shoes to shirts, dresses to jackets, much of our apparel lives in there. This is why it's important to give these hardworking garments a clean, and clean-smelling, environment to call home.

- Remove all items from the closet and set them aside before **sweeping or vacuuming** the **floor** of the closet, using the appropriate attachment.

- Lightly spray the **walls** of the closet using **All-Purpose Cleanser (page 18)**. Wipe up the spray, working top to bottom, with a **clean, lint-free cloth**.

- In a **small bowl**, mix ¼ **cup (60 mL) baking soda** with **5 to 10 drops essential oil of your choice** (I recommend **sandalwood or lavender**). Sprinkle the scented baking soda over the floor of the closet and let it sit for **30 minutes to 1 hour**. Vacuum up the baking soda and replace all your clothes and shoes.

Dresser Drawer Freshener

Dresser drawers have it pretty easy when it comes to carrying the domestic burden—for the most part, they are home to clean clothes exclusively (unlike their long-suffering colleague, the poor laundry hamper, subjected to every soiled garment life can throw at it). Still a dresser drawer likes to smell its best, so spruce it up with one of these sachets.

NOTE: These sachets also work well in closets, hung from the clothes rod on a string.

~~~~~~~~~

RICE AND ESSENTIAL OIL

- In a **small bowl**, mix **½ cup (125 mL) uncooked rice** with **5 to 10 drops essential oil of your choice** (I recommend **lavender, sandalwood, or eucalyptus**). Using a **teaspoon**, fill an **empty sachet or loose-leaf tea bag** with the mixture and secure the drawstring at the top.

RICE AND DRIED HERBS AND SPICES

- In a **small bowl**, mix **¼ cup (60 mL) uncooked rice** with either **¼ cup (60 mL) dried herbs of your choice** (**dried lavender or rosemary** is a good place to start), **whole spices such as clove, allspice, or dried citrus peels**, or **small fragments of cinnamon stick**. Using a **teaspoon**, fill an **empty sachet or loose-leaf tea bag** with the mixture and secure the drawstring at the top.

CEDAR SHAVINGS

- No rice necessary with this one—the **cedar shavings** provide their own heft. Using a **teaspoon**, fill an **empty sachet or loose-leaf tea bag** with the wood shavings and secure the drawstring at the top.

Laundry Hamper Deodorizer

Every laundry hamper has war stories to tell—the ways in which our clothes can get soiled and become stinky are as infinite as the days are long. Alas, cleaning a hamper—whether it is made of duck canvas, woven sea grass, or wicker—can be tricky. Luckily it's a snap to deodorize by following this simple routine.

- Every time you empty a load of laundry into the **washing machine**, sprinkle **baking soda** over the bottom of the now-empty hamper. This will absorb any odors from the dirty clothes and bed linens, which in turn will carry off some of the old baking soda into the next load.

NOTE: If you'd like to add a scent, in a **small bowl** mix **2 tablespoons (30 mL) baking soda** with **2 drops essential oil of your choice** before sprinkling in the hamper.

Baby Toy Disinfectant

Like puppies and kittens, babies investigate their environment by putting things into their mouths. If you have young ones in this exploratory stage of development, consider giving those wooden, rubber, and plastic toys a quick disinfecting treatment **once per week**. After all, nothing picks up microbes from the environment like a drool-soaked baby toy.

● Soak the corner of a **clean, lint-free cloth** in **full-strength vinegar** and rub down any **toys made of wood, rubber, or plastic**. Let the toys sit for 10 minutes and then rub down the toys once more with a corner of the cloth soaked in water. Air-dry and return the toys to their rightful owners.

Diaper Pail Refresher

Babies are notorious for two types of behavior: choppy sleep patterns and going to the bathroom wherever they happen to be—sitting in your lap, eating a meal, sleeping in their crib, the list goes on. Thank goodness for diapers! But who spares a thought for the stinky pail where used diapers are stored before either being disposed of or washed? Here's a way to disinfect your diaper pail and keep it smelling as little as possible like the human waste that calls it home.

- Using a **hammer and nail**, poke holes in the **screw-on metal lid of a clean, resealable 8-ounce (250 mL) glass jar** or similar receptacle. Add **½ cup (125 mL) baking soda**, **½ cup (125 mL) salt**, and **15 to 20 drops essential oil** (I recommend **lemon, eucalyptus, or peppermint**) to the jar and toss to combine before replacing the lid. Sprinkle the scented mixture on the bottom of the diaper pail every time you change the liner, making sure to vacuum up the previous baking soda first.

Zipper "Unsticker"

Sometimes the zippers on your luggage and clothing will become sticky or stiff over time, making them difficult to open and close (and increasing the likelihood that they will break). This is an easy fix, but **it does not work if there is fabric caught in the zipper—** that still has to be carefully and patiently worked out by hand.

- First, zip the **zipper** shut. Dip a **cotton swab** into **olive oil** and rub it over both sides of the zipper, reapplying oil to the swab as necessary and being careful to keep the oil away from any fabric. Open and close the zipper a couple of times to distribute the oil in the mechanism, then open the zipper and blot away any excess oil with a **paper towel or clean cloth**.

Leather Salt Stain Remover

If you wear leather shoes or boots in the winter, you are familiar with the ghostly white stains that appear on the sides after the leather dries. These are salt stains, a consequence of the widespread use of rock salt to melt ice and snow (see **Sidewalk De-Icer, page 215**, to learn how). When the water containing the dissolved salt dries, it leaves the salt behind in the leather. Here's how to clean these stains.

- Scrub the **footwear** well with a **stiff-bristled brush** to scrape away any dirt or caked-on salt.

- Soak the corner of a **clean, lint-free cloth** with **full-strength vinegar** and use it to rub at the remaining salt stain. When the stain has been lifted, use a **dry corner of the cloth** to soak up the vinegar you've applied to the leather and immediately condition with **Leather Conditioner (page 109)**.

Leather Conditioner

Because leather is made from the skin of an animal, it suffers in the same way our own skin does when it dries out: it becomes papery and flaky and will eventually crack. To keep your quality leather goods as supple and smooth as a second skin, regularly treat them to a little moisturizing therapy—especially during the winter months, when low humidity and occasional (or regular) snowfalls can take a toll.

- If the **leather** you are treating is a **shoe or boot**, begin by scrubbing the footwear well with a **stiff-bristled brush** to scrape away any caked-on dirt, and use a **damp, lint-free cloth** to clean the leather.

- Scoop up a dab of **coconut oil** with the corner of a **clean microfiber cloth** and rub it firmly and evenly over the surface of the leather. Make sure to apply the oil consistently or the leather may wind up with a blotchy appearance. Allow the leather to air-dry for **1 hour**, then buff to a dull shine with a **damp, lint-free cloth**.

NOTE: The leather will darken a little, so you may want to avoid using this treatment on white or very pale leathers.

Patent Leather Polish

Patent leather is produced by covering fine-grain leather with a glossy, protective coating. The method was invented at the end of the eighteenth century in Europe and introduced to the United States in 1819 by a New Jersey shoemaker named Seth Boyden, who used a special application based on linseed oil to achieve a high shine. Today that shine is achieved through plastics or synthetic resins. No matter how patent leather is made, this is the way to keep it looking its best.

NOTE: This also works for vinyl goods, so give those thigh-high boots and handbags an extra gleam while you're at it.

- Dip the corner of a **clean, microfiber cloth** into **full-strength vinegar** and polish the **patent leather or vinyl**, scrubbing at any scuff marks or stains. Then, use a **clean, dry, lint-free cloth** to buff the leather or vinyl to a high shine.

White Canvas Sneaker Brightener

One of the pillars of any wardrobe is the white canvas shoe or sneaker, an accessory that goes with countless outfits. This only applies if the shoes are as clean as possible, however—the downside of the white canvas shoe's versatility as a fashion staple is that it gets dirty easily. Use this trick to get your white canvas shoes runway-ready.

- Start by tackling the trouble spots. In a **small bowl**, mix **1 tablespoon (15 mL) baking soda** with **1 tablespoon (15 mL) water** to make a paste. Dip an **old toothbrush** into this mixture and scrub the dirtiest parts of the **shoe**, leaving the paste to dry. After about **1 hour**, scrape away the dried baking soda.

- Rinse out the bowl and mix **1 cup (250 mL) water** with ⅓ cup **(85 mL) strained lemon juice**. Dip the corner of a **clean, lint-free cloth** into the mixture and rub down the entire surface of the shoe, reapplying as necessary. Rinse the cloth and wring it out until just damp before using it to wipe the exterior of the shoe. Air-dry before wearing.

Shoe Deodorizer

All feet smell. Many feet smell bad. Some feet smell so bad, they make the hopper of a garbage truck at the end of its run smell like a spring day in a forest meadow. In other words, every shoe needs to be deodorized, at least a little bit (and some, a ton). Luckily baking soda is here to help.

- Sprinkle the insides of your smelly **shoes** liberally with **baking soda**, shaking to distribute and making sure you add enough to **cover the insoles and get into the toe box**. Leave the baking soda in the shoe for at least **24 hours**, but for as long as **1 week**. Before slipping them on, **vacuum** the insides of your shoes to remove the baking soda.

NOTE: If you'd like to use a scented deodorant option, in a **small bowl** toss ½ **cup (125 mL) baking soda** with **5 to 10 drops essential oil** (I recommend **lemon, eucalyptus, or peppermint**) before sprinkling it in your shoes.

Humidifier Cleanse

Whether you live in a warm-weather environment, where the air-conditioning is always on, or in a cold-weather environment, where forced heat is necessary to survive, a bedroom humidifier keeps your nasal passages from drying out while you sleep (which in turn helps you sleep better). Because humidifiers are warm, moist environments, they are an ideal home for mold and all sorts of bacteria. To prevent the buildup of unwanted microbes in the air you breathe, clean your humidifier once per week if you are using it every night.

* Unplug the **humidifier** and remove the **water tank**, pouring out any remaining water.

* Remove the cap from the tank and fill with **cool water** and ¼ cup **(60 mL) white vinegar**. Wipe down the cap with a **clean, lint-free cloth soaked in vinegar** and replace the cap. Dip the cloth in vinegar again and wipe down the top of the upturned tank, getting into all the nooks and crannies around the cap.

* Flip the tank back down and seat it in the base of the humidifier, letting the vinegar-water flow into the base. Let the humidifier stand like this for **30 minutes** before draining the tank and the base into the sink.

* Using an **old toothbrush or microfiber towel dipped in white vinegar**, scrub the water reservoir in the base of the humidifier, making sure to get into all the crevices. When the base has been scrubbed clean, wipe up the dislodged mold and bacteria with a **dry, lint-free cloth**.

* Refill the tank with **cool water** and run **once** during the day to eliminate any lingering vinegar odor before using it at night.

CHAPTER 5

THE BATHROOM

Aside from the front door, the bathroom door is the most likely to be locked in any home. This is because in the bathroom we are frequently at our most vulnerable, engaged in such highly personal activities as shaving our legs, cleaning our ears, and holding court on the porcelain throne, to name just three. Of all the rooms in the home, the bathroom perhaps deserves our deepest gratitude and our most sincere condolences. For it is here that we shed the worst parts of our physical selves in order to emerge, transformed, ready for whatever life brings us. And the bathroom just sits there and takes it, keeping some of our closest secrets safe and asking for very little in return. The recipes in this chapter are perfect for showing your bathroom how much you appreciate it for all the many favors it has done for you.

Bathroom Sink and Bathtub Drain Clog Remover

Most clogged drains begin with hair trapped in the pipe, close to the drain opening. The hair then traps other materials, such as fingernails, dirt, and soap scum, and so the clog grows over time. If you notice the water in your sink or tub draining more slowly than usual, clear the blockage before it becomes a bigger problem.

- First, attempt to remove the clog with a homemade drain snake: Take either a **medium zip tie** (for a sink drain) or a **large zip tie** (for a bathtub drain) and, using a **carpet knife or sharp wire-cutters**, cut three or four parallel lines about **1½ inches (4 cm)** apart on one side of the zip tie, starting at the tip. The cuts should be shallow, not past the halfway point of the zip tie, on a shallow angle that creates backward-facing barbs. Alternate similar cuts on the other side of the zip tie, in between the first set of cuts. Dip this homemade clog grabber down the **drain** and behold the horrors you draw forth from its murky recesses. Repeat as necessary.

- If the drain is still a little sluggish, there might be more material beyond the reach of your zip tie drain snake. Try flushing the remaining clog like this: Pour **½ cup (125 mL) salt** into the clogged drain and wash it down with **1 gallon (4 L) of very hot (not boiling) water**.

- And if that doesn't work, it's time to try a more potent solution: Mix **1 cup (250 mL) salt** with **1 cup (250 mL) baking soda** and pour into and around the clogged drain. Then pour **½ cup (125 mL) white vinegar** down the drain and let the mixture foam. After **10 minutes**, pour **1 gallon (4 L) boiling water** down the drain.

NOTE: If you have PVC (polyvinyl chloride, a type of plastic) pipes, or if you're not entirely sure what your pipes are made of, make sure the water is **very hot, but not boiling**. And whatever you do, **never use a plunger on a sink or tub drain**.

Shower Door Cleanser

You might think that because it's adjacent to lots of cleaning-up activities, a glass or heavy plastic shower door and divider should hardly ever need to be cleaned. But, in fact, this barrier is home to mold and bacteria and receives a steady barrage of soap scum, hair, and water splashes that need to be washed away regularly to keep the shower looking like the oasis it is.

NOTE: Get a **short-handled squeegee** and leave it in your bathtub or shower stall—it is an excellent tool for removing moisture from the shower door and divider, as long as it's used immediately after every shower.

- In a **small bowl**, mix **1 cup (250 mL) salt** and **1 cup (250 mL) baking soda**. Place **1 or 2 tablespoons (15 mL or 30 mL)** of the mixture onto a **large, damp sponge** and scour both sides of the **shower door and divider**, reapplying as necessary until you've covered the entire surface. Spray the paste-covered area with **All-Purpose Cleanser (page 18)** and rinse clean with a **clean sponge** and water.

Shower Mildew Preventer

Even the best ventilated shower will eventually see the spread of mold and mildew in the wettest areas. And in those bathrooms where there are no windows and the ventilation fan is on the fritz? That lucky shower is a hothouse, a place where one could raise a victory garden of mold. To slow the fungal parade, pre-treat the grout and tiles in trouble areas with this solution.

- Add **1 cup (250 mL) white vinegar** and **¼ cup (60 mL) salt** to a **small saucepan** and heat it over **medium** until the salt dissolves. When the mixture is cool to the touch, use a **small funnel** to pour it into a **clean 8-ounce (250 mL) glass spray bottle**. Replace the spray nozzle and store next to the shower. **Every couple of days**, when the walls of the shower are dry, spray this mixture over the areas where mold and mildew grow.

Bathtub and Bathroom Sink Cleanser

There are two main basins in the bathroom where we wash the remnants of the day from our faces, mouths, and bodies: the sink and the bathtub (or the shower, if you have a stand-alone). In the process we leave behind all manner of waste: hair, skin flakes, soap scum, toothpaste, shaving cream, and . . . other stuff. Here's how to keep these temples of cleanliness in tip-top shape.

- Run a **clean, damp sponge** over the area to be cleaned. Depending on the size of the basin you are cleaning, use a **flour sifter or fine-mesh stainless-steel strainer** to sprinkle **¼ cup to ½ cup (60 mL to 125 mL) baking soda**, coating the entire surface. Wrap **half a lemon in cheesecloth** and scour the **bathtub or sink**, using the cut end as your scrubbing surface. Rinse afterward with **cold water**.

Bathtub Ring Cleaner

If bath time in your home is a sacred ritual of personal renewal, you are familiar with the telltale ring of soap scum each use leaves behind. Once you've completed your ablutions and gotten dressed, it's time to clean that ring. Or, if the last person who used the tub is not as conscientious, you may have to do this *before* you draw your bath.

● In a **small saucepan**, mix **½ cup (125 mL) white vinegar** and **2 tablespoons (30 mL) salt** and heat on **high**, stirring until the salt has dissolved. Turn off the heat and pour the mixture into a **small bowl**. When the vinegar–salt mixture is cool enough to handle, bring it to the bathroom. Dip a **clean sponge** into the mixture and, using the scouring side, scrub away the bathtub ring, reapplying more cleanser as necessary. Store any leftover cleaner in a **small, resealable glass jar** or **glass spray bottle**.

Grout Stain Remover

The grout between tiles are the worry lines of the bathroom, revealing the weight of the world the tiles carry on their tiny ceramic or glass shoulders. Because the walls around the bathtub and shower tend to be highly humidified several times a day, mold and bacteria love to start new colonies nestled in the cracks between those tiles. To keep these worry lines from growing into something much worse, let salt and lemons come to the rescue.

- In a **small bowl**, mix **1 cup (250 mL) strained lemon juice** and **1 cup (250 mL) salt**. Apply the paste to the **grout** with a **clean, damp sponge**, pressing it into the cracks and scooping up more paste as necessary. With a **stiff scrub brush**, scour every vertical and horizontal line of grout, focusing on the trouble areas around the faucet handles and under the showerhead or wherever mold has begun to grow. Rinse with **cold water**.

Toilet Bowl Cleanser

Urban myth has it that the modern toilet was invented by a nineteenth-century plumbing wizard from London named Thomas Crapper, but that is not true—that honor goes to late-sixteenth-century royal Sir John Harington, a Scot whose godmother was Queen Elizabeth I. But Crapper got rich off his perfected toilets, which became widely used in England in the early twentieth century, when American servicemen serving overseas during World War I used his brand of commode and made the name synonymous with the device itself. Then, as now, toilets need to be cleaned regularly. Here's how.

- Pour **½ cup (125 mL) salt** and **1 cup (250 mL) baking soda** directly into your **toilet bowl**, making sure to get some on the sides. Then quickly pour **2 cups (500 mL) white vinegar** into the bowl, which will cause the foam to rise up the sides. Let this mixture stand for **30 minutes** before scrubbing the toilet bowl with a **toilet brush**. Flush once or twice to rinse away the last of the cleanser.

Toilet Bowl Stain Remover

If you live in an area with "hard" (that is, highly mineralized) water, your toilet may develop persistent limescale stains along the water line. These unsightly stains are not unusual, but they don't look great. If regular cleaning **(Toilet Bowl Cleanser, page 123)** doesn't work, try this solution.

● Find the **cutoff valve** for the toilet and close it. Once the water supply is off, flush the toilet to empty the bowl of any standing water. In a **small bowl**, mix ¼ cup (60 mL) salt and ¼ cup (60 mL) **baking soda**. Sprinkle this mixture liberally onto the stain and let it sit for **15 minutes**. Wearing **rubber or latex gloves** and using a **clean, damp sponge with a scouring pad**, scrub the stain clean. If the stain persists, dip the sponge into the remainder of your homemade scouring powder and give the bowl another going over. When the stain is gone, open the cutoff valve, let the tank refill, and flush away the residue.

Toilet Bowl Deodorizer

The modern latrine does a remarkable job of accepting and flushing away our worst-smelling waste, but it can only do so much when it comes to masking the smelly evidence of what's been done to it. Help your toilet (and the person who uses it after you) cope, using a couple of spritzes of this simple spray after every movement.

- Using a **small funnel**, pour **¼ cup (60 mL) 70 percent isopropyl alcohol** into a **clean 4-ounce (125 mL) glass spray bottle**. Add **15 to 20 drops essential oil of your choice (eucalyptus, lavender, and orange** work well) to the alcohol and gently swirl the bottle to mix. Finally, top up the bottle with water and replace the spray cap. Give the mixture a shake and set it out next to the toilet, ready to be used after every download.

Slate Tile Reviver

If you have slate tiles on your bathroom floor, you are familiar with their natural, rough-hewn charms. But you are probably also familiar with the way they can develop a powdery coating and start to look a little dingy. As a natural, untreated stone, slate is porous and absorbent, so it will accumulate dirt quickly. Here's a way to make it shine and protect it from further discoloration.

- First, **sweep** your **slate floor** to remove any dirt and dust.

- Then, fill a **small bucket** with **hot water** and, using a **large, clean sponge**, mop up the floor, starting away from the door and backing your way toward it. Turn on the **vent fan** and wait for the floor to dry.

- Fill a **small bowl** with **olive oil** and, using a **clean, microfiber towel or other lint-free cloth**, rub the oil into the floor, reapplying as necessary. As before, start away from the door and back your way toward it. Allow the oil to soak in for **30 minutes** before walking on the floor.

Toothbrush Reconditioner

Before it's time to send your toothbrush on to its second life as an appliance-scrubbing tool, consider reconditioning it to extend its life as your tooth-scrubbing tool. Especially if your toothbrush is made of plastic (as, let's face it, most of them are), getting the longest use out of it you can is better for the planet *and* for your wallet.

● In a **small saucepan**, mix **½ cup (125 mL) water** and **2 tablespoons (30 mL) salt** and heat on **high**, stirring until the salt has dissolved. Turn off the heat. When the mixture is cool enough to touch, pour it into a **12-ounce (375 mL) drinking glass**. Pop your toothbrush into the mixture, head down, and let it stand for **1 hour** before rinsing and storing.

NOTE: If you have a cold, substitute **white vinegar** for the water and follow these steps to keep your toothbrush germ-free until you're feeling better.

Hairbrush and Comb Cleaner

Your hairbrush and comb are doing yeoman's work every day, keeping your locks in place—nothing says "I got this" like a tidy head of hair. To keep these trusty implements free of skin flakes, dandruff, and other unwanted materials, follow this simple ritual **once per week**.

- Pull any strands of hair from your **brush or comb** and discard. Then, over a **medium bowl**, sprinkle your tools on both sides with **baking soda**. Pour a little **white vinegar** over the comb or brush to start the foaming action. When the foaming subsides, rinse thoroughly under **cold water**.

WHO Antimicrobial Spray

The World Health Organization was formed in response to the horrors of World War II as a public health organization dedicated to improving the well-being of the world's inhabitants by battling outbreaks of disease, directing medical aid to nations in need, and improving access to health care for everyone. Disclaimer: the WHO didn't invent this *exact* spray, but its contents are based on the organization's antimicrobial guidelines. Use it to treat the surfaces in your home when someone is sick to prevent the illness from spreading.

- Using a **small funnel**, pour **12 ounces (375 mL) 70 percent isopropyl alcohol** into a **clean 16-ounce (500 mL) glass spray bottle**. Add **2 tablespoons (30 mL) 3 percent hydrogen peroxide** and **15 to 20 drops essential oil of your choice (eucalyptus, peppermint, and lemongrass** all work well for this purpose). Replace the spray nozzle and shake well before every use.

CHAPTER 6

THE LAUNDRY

Doing laundry gives us an opportunity to reflect on the events of the past few days of our lives. As we pick up and sort each piece on its way to the washer or from the dryer or clothesline, we are reminded of when we wore that garment, the places we visited, and the people we saw. It is, in effect, an opportunity for meditation. Or, and I write these words in order to embrace the full spectrum of human experience, laundry is a dreaded, repetitive chore that has the unique ability to ruin what would have otherwise been a perfectly lovely day doing something else. Whatever your feelings are about this common household chore, it is an undeniable necessity. Here are some tricks to make your moments of reflection even more relaxed—or your time in the dirty-clothes gulag that much less taxing.

Stain Pretreatments

There are two kinds of stains—the kind you notice as it happens and the kind you don't realize is there until much later. It's always better to clean a stain that has just happened, before it dries and becomes permanently fixed in the weave of the fabric, but these suggestions for pretreating several common varieties of stains work on stains old and new.

NOTE: When cleaning stained clothing, always use **cold water**—if the stain doesn't come out, you'll be able to try again; use hot water and you risk setting the stain for good.

SWEAT STAINS

- For white shirts: In a **small bowl**, mix **2 tablespoons (30 mL) baking soda** and **2 tablespoons (30 mL) hydrogen peroxide** to make a paste, scaling up these quantities as necessary. Rub the paste on the affected areas before washing.

- For dark shirts: Soak in a mixture of **1 part white vinegar to 8 parts cold water** for **30 minutes** before washing.

BLOOD STAINS

- If the stain is fresh, dab any blood with a **clean, dry rag or paper towel**. Rinse the stain under **cold water** and then, using your fingertip, rub **Castile soap** into the stain before washing.

COFFEE AND TEA STAINS

- If the stain is still wet, dab with a **clean, dry rag or paper towel**. Rinse the stain under **cold water** and then, using your fingertip, rub **Castile soap** into the stain. Rinse again. If the stain is still visible, soak in a mixture of **1 part white vinegar to 8 parts cold water** for **30 minutes** before washing.

WINE STAINS

- If the stain is still wet, dab with a **clean, dry rag or paper towel**. Pour a small mound of **table salt** over the stain and add a **few drops of water**. Wait until the salt dries, around **1 hour**. Brush the salt off and wash.

GRASS STAINS

- In a **small bowl**, mix **1 part white vinegar to 2 parts water**. Soak the affected area of clothing in this mixture for **30 minutes**. Rinse. Apply a dab of **Castile soap** to the stain with your fingertip and rub into the affected area. Wait **15 minutes** before washing.

INK STAINS

- Place a **clean, dry rag or paper towel** underneath the ink stain. Dip the end of a cotton swab in **70 percent isopropyl alcohol** and rub out the stain before washing.

OILY STAINS

- Apply a dab of **Castile soap** to the stain with your fingertip and firmly scrub the stain on both sides of the fabric. Rinse with **cold water** and soak the affected area in a mixture of **1 part vinegar to 1 part water**. Wait **15 minutes** before washing.

Laundry Booster

If you're throwing a load of especially dirty laundry into the washing machine, give your regular detergent a boost with this simple addition.

- Add **½ cup (125 mL) baking soda** along with the detergent at the start of the wash cycle.

Laundry Deodorizer

If you have a load of laundry that, speaking frankly, stinks—dirty underwear, hard-used socks, and children's clothing of any kind, for instance—use this simple method to ensure those foul-smelling clothes emerge from the wash odor-free.

- If you have a **top-loading machine**, load the laundry, add the detergent, and wash as usual. Stop the machine at the **rinse cycle** and add **1 cup (250 mL) white vinegar**. Wait **15 minutes** before closing the lid and restarting the machine.

- If you have a **front-loading machine**, pour the vinegar into the bleach dispenser and run the wash cycle.

Laundry Softener

There are a couple of benefits to using a laundry softener, besides the obvious: it helps reduce wrinkling and reduces friction in the fibers, resulting in less wear and tear on clothes over time. Commercial softeners and dryer sheets do a good job at these tasks, but they also leave a fine, oily residue behind. For most clothing this is not a problem, but in technical fabrics of the sort athletic garments are made of, this residue can compromise its moisture-wicking properties. This residue can also make white clothes look a little dingy. Happily this homemade preparation is suitable for all kinds of fabric.

~~~~~~~~~

● In a **clean, resealable 16-ounce (500 mL) glass jar**, thoroughly mix **¾ cup (375 mL) Epsom salt** with **¾ cup (375 mL) baking soda**. Add **2 tablespoons (30 mL)** of this mixture to each load when you add the detergent.

White Load Lightener

Part of the joy of wearing white clothes lies in their unblemished, light-reflecting qualities. And don't get me started on the glories of perfectly white bed linens! Sadly, the indignity of existing in a world filled with dirt and sweat can dampen that joy by graying our whites. Here's how to keep these garments and bedclothes bright.

~~~~~~~~~

- If you have a **top-loading machine**, add **1 cup (250 mL) hydrogen peroxide** as the water fills but before you add the clothes. Allow the load to soak in the treated water for **15 minutes** before closing the lid and restarting the cycle.

- If you have a **front-loading machine**, pour **½ cup (125 mL) hydrogen peroxide** into the bleach dispenser and run the wash cycle.

Color Load Brightener

It can be harder to tell with colored clothes, but they get dingy too. Their once-vibrant hues begin to look more subdued as time passes, in part because of dirt lodged in the fibers and in part because of the residue left behind by detergents. To restore them to their colorful natures, try this.

● If you have a **top-loading machine**, add **1 cup (250 mL) white vinegar** and **2 tablespoons (30 mL) salt** as it is filling, but before you add the clothes. Allow the load to soak in the treated water for **15 minutes** before closing the lid and restarting the cycle.

● If you have a **front-loading machine**, pour **1 tablespoon (15 mL) salt** and **½ cup (125 mL) white vinegar** into the bleach dispenser and run the wash cycle.

Vinyl Shower Curtain
Liner Cleanse

The vinyl shower curtain liner is the red-headed stepchild of the bathroom. Always kept hidden behind its fashion-forward sister, the regular shower curtain, the liner is kept in the dark and splashed with water, soap scum, and who knows what else on a daily basis. Unfortunately all that moisture and residue promote mold and mildew growth. The good news is that it can be washed before being sent back to its room without dinner.

- Using the **All-Purpose Cleanser (page 18)**, pretreat by spraying the inside of the **shower curtain liner** while it is still hanging from the rod. Remove the liner from the rings and put it in the **washing machine** with a load of rags. Add the **detergent** and **1 cup (250 mL) white vinegar** and run on the gentle cycle. Line dry.

Line-Dried Clothing Anti-Freeze

If you like to line-dry your clothing even when the weather hits the freezing mark, this trick will help keep your shirts and pants from stiffening into boards as they dry. Of course, if the temperature dips below 15 degrees F (–9 degrees C) or so, no amount of salt in the water is going to help keep the clothes from freezing.

● Add **1 cup (250 mL) salt** to your **washing machine** during the rinse cycle. The addition of salt lowers the freezing temperature of water.

Swimsuit Reconditioner

Over the course of a bright, sunny day spent in a chlorine-treated pool, swimsuits are subjected to all sorts of factors that threaten the vibrancy of their color. This simple reconditioning technique, which relies on vinegar, takes advantage of the fact that the dyes used in swimsuit manufacturing are acidic in nature. Most laundry detergents are bases, so if you want to extend the life of your swimsuit, go with this low-pH solution instead and keep your suit out of the washing machine.

- Fill your bathroom sink with water and add **3 tablespoons (45 mL) white vinegar**. Add your swimsuit to the vinegar-water and allow it to soak for **1 hour**. Drain the sink and thoroughly rinse the swimsuit with **cold water** before air-drying. Your swimsuit is now ready for another day at the pool.

Linen Spray

Linen spray is a household hack most people didn't realize they needed in their lives until they tried it or experienced it in someone else's home. This quick-drying spray is used primarily to keep linens stored in closets and drawers smelling fresh, no matter how long they're in there. But it is actually an aromatherapy multitasker: spray onto your active bedlinens, pillows, and towels, or spritz inside a teenager's musty bedroom or smelly car. Best of all, it has none of the toxic ingredients (benzene, formaldehyde, and various phthalates, to name just a few) of many synthetic commercial products.

- In a **small bowl**, combine ⅓ **cup (80 mL) high-proof vodka or 70 percent isopropyl alcohol** and **40 drops essential oil of your choice** (coming up with your custom scent combination is the fun part of this recipe, but to get you started I recommend **20 drops cedarwood, 15 drops rosemary, and 5 drops grapefruit**). In a **separate small bowl**, stir **1 teaspoon (5 mL) fine sea salt** and ⅓ **cup warm, distilled water** until the salt dissolves. Add the salt water to the alcohol mixture and stir to combine. Using a **small funnel**, pour the mixture into a **clean 8-ounce (250 mL) glass spray bottle**, replace the spray nozzle, and shake well before every use.

NOTE: Use this spray after you iron and before you fold your linens. If you have linens that rarely see use—sheets and coverlets for a guest bed, for instance—spray **once per month** to keep them and the storage space smelling their best.

Steam Iron Reconditioner

The humble clothes iron, a superheated slab of metal used to reorient the cellulose fibers in clothing, seems like an appliance that would be immune to damage from the garments it flattens. In reality, all sorts of substances are transferred to the surface of the iron, which over time can make it slightly "sticky." To keep your iron as frictionless as possible, follow this simple reconditioning technique.

- While your **iron** is heating up, place a sturdy piece of paper on your ironing board. Sprinkle the paper with a coating of **coarse salt** and iron the salt crystals with **no steam**, using a steady circular motion, for **2 minutes**. As you iron, make sure the entire surface of the device comes into contact with the salt crystals. Discard the paper and salt.

Steam Iron Tank Cleanser

Like all heated-water appliances, the tank and water line of your clothes iron can develop mineral scale over time. To clean it, follow this simple procedure.

- Fill the **water reservoir** of your **steam iron** with **one-half water** and **one-half white vinegar**. Once the iron has heated up, set to steam and allow the iron to sit for **5 minutes**. Drain the tank and refill it with **plain cold water**. Once the iron has heated up again, place a **sturdy rag** on your **ironing board** and steam iron it until the tank is empty. Refill the tank one more time and your iron is ready to tackle the next round of wrinkly clothes.

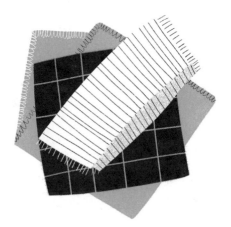

CHAPTER 7

THE PERSONAL TOUCH

Feeling good and looking good have been essential to human well-being for as far back as records exist. The ancient Ayurvedic texts, for example, suggest citrus to calm the nerves. In ancient Egypt, Dead Sea salt was used as an exfoliant to brighten and soften the skin. And traditional Chinese medicine has recommended ginger as a treatment for nausea and upset stomach for two thousand years.

In this chapter, you'll find lots of practical preparations drawn from these and more modern traditions that will make you look and feel better. And although most of the recipes here include at least one of our starring ingredients (salt, lemons, vinegar, or baking soda), a handful rely solely on a cast of the supporting players mentioned in Chapter 1. Finally, a note of caution: **Do not use any ingredients to which you are allergic in these health and cosmetic treatments. If you're not sure about potential allergies, try a small application on the skin of your forearm, and wait 5 minutes to see if you have a reaction.**

Steam Facial

Steam treatments are a great way to clean away dead skin, moisturize, open the pores, prevent or treat existing acne, and increase blood flow to the skin (which promotes the production of collagen and elastin, two proteins responsible for firmness and resiliency). The process couldn't be simpler.

- **Boil 1 quart (4 L) water** in a **large pot** and pour it into a **large, wide bowl**. Add either **10 drops essential oil** (**eucalyptus** to open pores, **chamomile** for sensitive skin, **rosemary** for oily skin, and **orange or grapefruit** for the sheer joy of it), **1 lemon or orange, cut into slices**, or **2 tablespoons (30 mL) dried herbs of your choice** and let the water cool for **5 minutes**. Place your head, face down and eyes closed, over the bowl and drape a **clean dish towel** over your head, creating a loose seal around the edge. If the heat is too much, move your face farther away. Steam for at least **5 minutes** and up to **10 minutes**.

- Then, while your pores are open, gently exfoliate your skin with **Exfoliating Sugar Scrub (page 150)** or **Gentle Exfoliating Facial Scrub (page 151)**.

Exfoliating Salt Scrub

Our skin is the living barrier that protects us from the outside world as well as the largest single organ in the human body. As our birthday suit of armor, skin gets covered in dirt, sweat, harmful bacteria, and all sorts of other contaminants—including dead skin cells. To keep your skin clean and tight and your pores clear, you don't have to purchase an expensive product—try this simple, effective scrub instead.

NOTE: Use **no more than every two or three days**; your skin's natural chemistry and colonies of beneficial bacteria need time to rebalance in between treatments.

- In a **medium bowl**, mix **1 cup (250 mL) fine sea salt, ¼ cup (60 mL) olive oil, 10 drops lemon essential oil (or other scent of your choice)**, and **1 tablespoon (15 mL) dried thyme (or other dried herb of your choice)**. Place the mixture in a **clean, resealable glass jar**. Before you step out of your next bath or shower, apply a handful of this fragrant salt scrub to your skin, moving your palms in a circular motion. When you are done, rinse any residue away with **cool water**. Sea salt crystals are quite angular, by the way, so this preparation is **best used on your body and not your face**.

Exfoliating Sugar Scrub

If you have particularly sensitive skin, or if you are exfoliating your face, you may want to use a sugar-based scrub instead of the **Exfoliating Salt Scrub (page 149)**. Sugar granules are easier on the skin because they are rounder than sea salt granules and dissolve more quickly when they come into contact with water. In general **you should not use a physical exfoliant such as salt or sugar more than two or three times per week**.

NOTE: Because it is loaded with minerals that are good for your skin, unrefined cane sugar makes an excellent scrub too, but it is quite angular and coarse, so it may be better suited to your body than your face if you have sensitive skin.

- In a **medium bowl**, mix **1 cup (250 mL) table sugar, ¼ cup (60 mL) virgin coconut oil, 5 drops lemon essential oil (or other scent of your choice)**, and **1 tablespoon (15 mL) fine citrus zest (lemon, orange, or grapefruit work well)**. Place the mixture in a **clean, resealable glass jar**. Before you step out of your next bath or shower, or after you wash your face at the sink, apply a handful of sugar scrub to your skin, rubbing gently using a circular motion. When you are done, rinse away any residue with **cool water**.

Gentle Exfoliating Facial Scrub

For particularly sensitive or acne-prone skin, this scrub is a softer, gentler alternative to the **Exfoliating Sugar Scrub (page 150)** because it uses rice flour, which has smaller granules than table sugar.

- In a **small bowl**, mix ¼ **cup (60 mL) rice flour**, **2 tablespoons (30 mL) honey**, **1 tablespoon (15 mL) distilled water**, and **1 teaspoon (5 mL) argan oil**. Store the mixture in a **clean, resealable glass jar**. Apply to your face with your fingertips, rubbing gently in a circular motion. Rinse thoroughly and don't forget to apply moisturizer afterward.

Skin-Softening Bath Salts

The practice of bathing in hot springs is an ancient one, common among cultures with access to these naturally heated, mineral-rich water features. (Even snow monkeys, the famed Japanese macaques, make use of hot springs, allowing them to extend their range farther north than any other nonhuman primate.) Thanks to the miracles of modern plumbing and heating, we can emulate the cleaning and restorative powers of the hot spring in our homes with this quick recipe.

● The next time you draw a hot bath, pour **1 cup (250 mL) hand-harvested sea salt** (which is rich in minerals) and **½ cup (125 mL) baking soda** into the **running water**. Give the bath a big swirl to distribute. When the bath is ready, soak your bones for **30 minutes to 1 hour**. After you towel off, make sure to moisturize **(Body Lotion, page 155)**.

Fizzy, Lemon-Scented Bath Salts

This is a scented, effervescent variation of the **Skin-Softening Bath Salts (page 152)**—the sunny citrus aroma alone is worth the extra work.

- In a **medium bowl**, mix **½ cup (125 mL) baking soda**, **½ cup (125 mL) fine sea salt**, and **¼ cup (60 mL) cornstarch**. In a **small bowl**, mix **1 teaspoon (5 mL) virgin coconut oil**, **¼ cup (60 mL) strained lemon juice**, and **5 drops lemon essential oil**. Since the fizz is short-lived, you'll want to gather your ingredients and bring them to the bathtub, ready to use. Once the bath is drawn and you are in the water, add the wet ingredients to the dry ingredients and give a quick stir, then pour the foaming mixture directly into the bath with you. Soak in the lemon-scented water for up to **40 minutes**, allowing it to soften and cleanse your skin. After you towel off, seal in the moisturizing effect by applying a light lotion to your skin **(Body Lotion, page 155)**.

Moisturizing Honey-Milk Bath Soak

For an extra-moisturizing bath treatment, try this delightful mixture of three ingredients you almost certainly have in your kitchen right now. Honey contains numerous antioxidants and skin-softening amino acids, while milk features lactic acid, numerous proteins, and skin-nourishing fats. And sea salt contains many minerals that are beneficial to the skin, including calcium, magnesium, and potassium. Together they offer a moisturizing treat for dry skin.

- In a **small saucepan**, heat **2 cups (500 mL) whole milk, ½ cup (125 mL) fine sea salt**, and **1 cup (250 mL) buckwheat honey** (any honey will work, but darker honeys contain more beneficial nutrients), stirring until the honey has dissolved (and to prevent a "skin" from forming on the milk). Turn off the heat and pour this mixture into a drawn bath, giving the bath a big swirl to combine.

Body Lotion

Most commercial moisturizers are loaded with additives and can be very expensive (especially high-end brands). Luckily, it's a snap to make a customized, luxurious moisturizer at home for a fraction of the cost.

NOTE: Coconut oil becomes solid below 76 degrees F (24.5 degrees C), so you may want to warm it up on the stove or in the microwave to make the mixing process easier.

- In a **mixing bowl**, add **2 cups (500 mL) virgin coconut oil**. Whip the coconut oil with an **electric hand-mixer** until light and fluffy, **5 to 7 minutes**. If you'd like a scented moisturizer, add **10 to 20 drops essential oil** (**lavender and frankincense** are good choices) and crank up the hand-mixer for another **10 seconds**. Scoop your moisturizer into a **clean, resealable glass jar** and store in the bathroom.

NOTE: Coconut oil has a lovely, subtle aroma all on its own, so you may want to make this a one-ingredient recipe.

Skin Toner

After washing or exfoliating your face, tighten your pores again with this treatment made from a pantry staple: rice. This tonic contains helpful antioxidants (including inositol, a sugar manufactured by the human body), which are compounds known to prevent cell damage.

● In a **medium bowl**, mix **½ cup (125 mL) uncooked rice** with **1½ cups (375 mL) distilled water** and let sit for **1 hour**. Pour the rice-water through a **fine-mesh stainless-steel strainer** into a **clean, resealable glass jar** and store in the **refrigerator**. Dip a **cotton ball** into the chilled rice-water and massage it into your skin at the end of your skin care regime. Then you have a choice: rinse your skin with **cold water** or allow the rice-water to dry on your face.

Face-Moisturizing Serum

Because the skin on our faces tends to be more prone to acne, it is better to moisturize it using a noncomedogenic oil (that is, one that doesn't clog pores). This rules out coconut and olive oils, though both have many benefits to the skin (including antioxidants). In this simple preparation, it's argan oil to the rescue.

~~~~~~~~~~

● In a **small bowl**, mix **1 tablespoon (15 mL) argan oil**, **1 tablespoon (15 mL) aloe vera gel**, **½ teaspoon (2.5 mL) honey**, and **5 drops rosemary essential oil**. Using a **small funnel**, pour the mixture into a **clean 2-ounce (60 mL) glass dropper bottle**. Use **2 or 3 drops** applied with your fingertips to moisturize your skin after cleansing. Shake well before each use.

Shaving Cream

Slapping a handful of light, fluffy shaving cream onto your stubble is one of the most fun-for-its-own-sake activities in any beauty routine. But many shaving creams contain unnecessary chemical additives, and some come in environmentally unfriendly, aerosol-powered dispensers. Here's how to make one at home that is just as delightful to use, less harmful to the environment, and much more affordable.

NOTE: Coconut oil becomes solid below 76 degrees F (24.5 degrees C), so you may want to warm it up on the stove or in the microwave to make the mixing process easier.

- In a **medium bowl**, add ½ cup (125 mL) virgin coconut oil, **1 tablespoon (15 mL) extra-virgin olive oil**, and **2 teaspoons (10 mL) baking soda**. Whip this mixture with an **electric hand-mixer** until light and fluffy, **5 to 7 minutes**. Add **5 drops essential oil of your choice** (**sandalwood or eucalyptus** work well) and crank up the hand-mixer for another **10 seconds** to incorporate. Store your pre-fluffed shaving cream in a **clean, resealable glass jar** and store in the bathroom.

NOTE: If you are in a hurry, you can also simply apply **olive oil or coconut oil** to the skin before shaving.

Skin-Tightening Aftershave

Dragging a sharp blade at an angle across your skin is not without its dangers, especially as you navigate the curves of your face or the swooping contours of your legs. If you find yourself scratched and abraded after your last tussle with a razor, use this skin-tightening mixture afterward.

- In a **small bowl**, mix **3 tablespoons (45 mL) pure witch hazel**, **2 tablespoons (30 mL) aloe vera gel**, **1 tablespoon (15 mL) distilled water**, and **5 to 7 drops essential oil of your choice** (**rosemary or frankincense** work well here). Using a **small funnel**, pour the mixture into a **clean 2-ounce (60 mL) glass spray bottle**. Replace the nozzle and shake well before each use. Spritz lightly over affected skin (close your eyes if you are spraying your face).

Anti-Acne Facial Mask

As a teenager, I imagined adulthood as a land of plenty, full of wonderful new adventures, the thrill of true independence, and much less time spent with my parents. One thing I thought for sure would come to an end was acne. But now that I'm older and wiser, I know that pimples, like diamonds, are forever. Acne usually occurs when a follicle becomes blocked with oil and dead skin cells; add in common bacteria and the result is a pimple (or lots of them). Here's a mask that can help speed the healing process without damaging your skin when a breakout occurs. The antibacterial effect of the honey combined with the mild exfoliating properties of baking soda and the antioxidants in the citrus make this mask especially effective.

● In a **small bowl**, mix **2 tablespoons (30 mL) honey, 1 teaspoon (5 mL) lemon juice**, and **1 teaspoon (5 mL) baking soda**. Dab this slightly sticky mixture onto your skin with your fingertips, avoiding your eyes (if putting it on your face) and other sensitive areas, and allow it to remain in place for **10 minutes**. Rinse thoroughly with **warm water**, then **cold water**. Finally, moisturize with **Face-Moisturizing Serum (page 157)**.

Shampoo

Your hair type—fine or coarse, dry or oily, curly or straight, thick or thin—will determine how frequently you need to, or should, shampoo. This is because shampoo is a surfactant, which means it cuts through oil and lifts dirt and other debris from your hair and scalp. If you have oily hair, you may have to shampoo **every day or every other day**, but if you have thick, curly hair or very dry hair, you may need to shampoo just **once per week**. No matter what, you're going to want to wash your hair at some point, of course. This formula works well on all types of hair and is free from the cornucopia of strange and sometimes harsh chemicals found in nearly every commercial shampoo out there.

- In a **small bowl**, carefully mix ⅓ **cup (80 mL) Castile soap**, ⅓ **cup (80 mL) water**, **1 teaspoon (5 mL) olive oil**, and **10 to 15 drops essential oil of your choice** (**lemon and thyme or lemon and tea tree** are good places to start). Using a **small funnel**, pour into a **clean 8-ounce (250 mL) plastic squeeze bottle with a lid**. Swirl the bottle before each application to gently mix the ingredients.

NOTE: This shampoo is thinner than commercial varieties but lathers up nicely—a little bit goes a long way!

Dry Shampoo

If you have long hair, washing it is a multistage process—and it takes a minute too. Plus, the worst-kept secret in hair care is that daily washing with shampoo is bad for your scalp and your hair, stripping them of their natural oils and drying them out. If you are in a rush or trying to minimize shampoo-related damage to your hair, try this quick volumizing and freshening dry shampoo.

Below are four different combinations of ingredients, based on hair color, but the application process is the same: Leaning over the bathtub, flip your hair forward and, using a **flour sifter or fine-mesh stainless-steel strainer**, sprinkle the **dry shampoo** onto your hair. With your fingertips, work the shampoo powder throughout your hair, to the ends. Flip your hair back and sprinkle more on top of your hair before using a **brush or comb** to evenly distribute and remove any excess product. Then style as you normally would.

NOTE: For the tinted shampoos, add or subtract a little of the color-adding ingredient to match your personal hair color.

BLOND OR SILVER HAIR

- In a **small bowl**, mix ¼ cup (60 mL) cornstarch, ¼ cup (60 mL) **baking soda**, and **5 to 10 drops essential oil of your choice** (**lemongrass or frankincense** work well).

BROWN HAIR

- In a **small bowl**, mix ¼ cup (60 mL) cornstarch, 2 tablespoons (30 mL) baking soda, 2 tablespoons (30 mL) cacao powder (or **cocoa**, if that's all you have, but cacao is better because it is minimally processed and contains more nutrients), and **5 to 10 drops essential oil of your choice** (**lemongrass or frankincense** work well).

RED HAIR

- In a **small bowl**, mix ¼ **cup (60 mL) cornstarch**, **2 tablespoons (30 mL) baking soda**, **2 tablespoons (30 mL) cinnamon powder**, and **5 to 10 drops essential oil of your choice** (**lemongrass or frankincense** work well, even in combination with the cinnamon).

BLACK HAIR

- In a **small bowl**, mix ¼ **cup (60 mL) cornstarch**, **2 tablespoons (30 mL) baking soda**, **2 tablespoons (30 mL) activated charcoal powder**, and **5 to 10 drops essential oil of your choice** (**lemongrass or frankincense** work well).

Under-Eye Reviver

Many conditions can cause the skin under the eye to become looser, more wrinkled, and darker: lack of sleep, an unhealthy diet, illness, and the inexorable march of time. While you should, of course, try to address these contributing factors (well, not the passage of time—there's no cure for that), you can temporarily tighten up your under-eye skin with this quick fix, which is safe to use daily.

● In a **small saucepan**, heat **½ cup (125 mL) pure witch hazel** with **2 tablespoons (30 mL) salt**, stirring until the salt dissolves. Remove from the heat and allow to cool.

● Place **24 cotton balls** into a **medium bowl**. When the witch hazel solution has cooled, sprinkle it over the cotton balls until they are lightly soaked. Place the cotton balls into a **plastic sandwich bag** and store in the **freezer**. When you want to tighten the skin under your eyes, remove two cotton balls and hold one under each eye for **5 minutes**.

Conditioner

Shampooing washes away accumulated skin flakes, dandruff, and dirt, but it also strips your locks of their natural coating of protective oil, drying out your hair and scalp in the process. To prevent your hair from becoming brittle and frizzy (and your scalp from getting dry and itchy), use a conditioning treatment to restore some of that protection **one to three times per week**, depending on how often you shampoo and how naturally oily your hair is.

- In a **blender or food processor**, whip **¼ cup (60 mL) virgin coconut oil, 2 tablespoons (30 mL) olive oil, 1 tablespoon (15 mL) honey**, and **1 ripe banana** until smooth, around **2 minutes**. Scoop the conditioner into a **clean resealable 8-ounce (250 mL) glass jar**. To use, apply to wet, clean hair and let stand for **5 minutes** before rinsing.

NOTE: This will keep for **1 week** at room temperature and for **1 month** in the fridge (recommended if you live in a home where room temperature is higher than 76 degrees F or 24.5 degrees C).

Hair Deep-Conditioner

It's gross but true: hair consists of long strands of dead cells that have been pushed through the skin by hair follicles. And the job of sebaceous glands, which grow next to the hair follicles, is to keep hair strong and shiny by coating it with natural oils. Even though hair is not technically alive, our bodies work hard to keep it looking as *lively* as possible. Alas, due to various stressors—shampooing, blow-drying, chemical straightening, environmental pollution, sun exposure, the list goes on—those oils get stripped away and hair can become dry, brittle, and dirty. To repair damaged hair and enhance its shine, treat yourself to a deep conditioning before your next wash and your hair will thank you from the bottom of its little zombie heart.

- In a **small saucepan**, bring **¼ cup (60 mL) water** to a **boil** and remove from the heat. Let sit for **5 minutes**. In a **blender or food processor**, add the **boiled water, 2 tablespoons (30 mL) honey**, and **¼ cup (60 mL) olive oil**. Blend on high until the mixture has emulsified, then immediately pour into a **large coffee mug** and let it cool slightly until warm.

- Over the sink or bathtub, flip your hair forward and use your fingertips to massage approximately half the oil into your hair, from your scalp to the ends. Flip your hair back and work the rest of the oil into the hair on the top of your head. Immediately wrap your hair in an **old towel**. After **30 minutes**, remove the towel and wash your hair completely—you may need to wash it twice to remove the last of the oil. Dry and style as usual.

Beach Wave Inducer

If you have long, straight hair, you know that a day spent swimming in the ocean can leave you with a fuller, wavier, lighter-colored coif—beachy waves! This happens because sea salt cleans oil and dirt from your hair, adds body and minerals, and induces a slight curl, or wave. Try this simple solution to get the beachy look at home, but **don't use it more than two or three times per week**—any more than that and you risk drying out your hair and scalp.

~~~~~~~~~

- In a **small saucepan**, heat **1 cup (250 mL) water**, **1 chamomile tea bag**, and **1 tablespoon (15 mL) fine sea salt**, stirring until the salt has dissolved. Remove from heat and after **5 minutes**, discard the tea bag. Add **2 tablespoons (30 mL) aloe vera gel**, **2 teaspoons (10 mL) argan oil**, and **1 teaspoon (5 mL) strained lemon juice**. When the mixture is cool to the touch, use a **small funnel** to pour it into a **clean 12-ounce (375 mL) glass spray bottle** and replace the nozzle. Shake well before each use.

- After washing and towel-drying your hair, flip your hair forward and spray from the roots to the ends. Flip your hair back and spray the hair on the top of your head before using a **wide-toothed comb** to evenly distribute. Loosely scrunch your hair into a **shower cap** or a **large-toothed hair clip** and let it sit for **30 minutes**, or until dry.

NOTE: You may substitute **coconut oil** for the **argan oil**.

Hair Volumizer

For the finer-haired among us, adding body is a must. This can be accomplished through a variety of different treatments, but not all of them (for instance, **Beach Wave Inducer, page 167**) should be used every day. This volumizer, however, is perfectly safe for **daily use** and does an excellent job of fortifying your hair in its battle against gravity.

- In a **small bowl**, mix **1 cup (250 mL) water** and ½ **cup (125 mL) aloe vera gel**. Add **1 teaspoon (5 mL) coconut oil** and **5 drops essential oil of your choice** (**rosemary or lemongrass** work well) and stir to combine. Using a **small funnel**, pour the mixture into a **clean 16-ounce (500 mL) glass spray bottle** and replace the nozzle. Shake well before each use.

- After washing and towel-drying your hair, flip your hair forward and spray from the roots to the ends. Flip your hair back and spray the hair on the top of your head before using a **wide-toothed comb** to evenly distribute. Allow to air-dry.

Hair Color Lightener

Nature offers its own hair-bleaching treatment through exposure to the sun and (if you're lucky) the ocean. If you don't live near the sea or it's still months away from beach weather, you can still give yourself a touch of that just-back-from-the-beach hair color, whatever your seasonal motivation.

- In a **small saucepan, boil 1 cup (250 mL) water** and turn off the heat. Add **5 chamomile tea bags** and steep for **5 minutes**. Discard the tea bags and, using a **small funnel**, pour **½ cup (125 mL) concentrated chamomile tea** into a **clean 8-ounce (250 mL) glass spray bottle**. Add **½ cup (125 mL) strained lemon juice** (the juice from about 3 or 4 lemons) and replace the nozzle.

- After washing and towel-drying your hair, flip your hair forward and spray from the roots to the ends. Flip your hair back and spray the hair on the top of your head before using a **wide-toothed comb** to evenly distribute. Allow to air-dry.

NOTE: Exposure to the sun will accelerate the hair-lightening process, but no matter what, it will take several treatments for the effects to be noticeable. **Do not use for more than a month at a time** as the lemon juice will have a drying effect that can leave your hair brittle and with a tendency toward frizz.

Anti-Dandruff Treatment

Dandruff, a type of seborrheic dermatitis (flaky skin irritation, in plain language), happens to many people, from infancy (when it is called "cradle cap") through adulthood. It isn't dangerous or contagious, but it can make your scalp itch, and the flakes don't look great in your hair or scattered across your shoulders. Dandruff seems to be caused by a variety of factors, including the presence of yeast in the genus *Malassezia* (various species of which cause several unpleasant skin conditions), an excess of oil (which these yeast feed on), stress, low humidity, shampooing too frequently or not frequently enough, and chemical sensitivity. Dandruff can't be cured, exactly, but it can be treated using common household staples.

APPLE CIDER VINEGAR RINSE FOR OILY HAIR AND SCALP

- In a **small bowl**, add ¼ cup (60 mL) water, **1 tablespoon (15 mL) apple cider vinegar**, and **5 drops rosemary essential oil**. Over the bathtub, flip your **hair** forward and use your fingertips to work approximately half the rinse into your hair, from your scalp to the ends. Flip your hair back and work the remainder of the vinegar rinse into your hair, starting from your hairline and working toward the back. Wait **10 minutes**, then rinse with **cool water** before shampooing and conditioning.

COCONUT OIL MASK FOR DRY HAIR AND SCALP

- In a **small bowl**, mix ¼ cup (60 mL) **coconut oil** with **5 drops tea tree essential oil**. Over the bathtub, flip your hair forward and use your fingertips to massage approximately half the oil into your hair, from your scalp to the ends. Flip your hair back and work the remainder of the oil into the hair on the top of your head. Wait **1 hour**, then shampoo and rinse thoroughly before styling.

Lip Balm

Because the thin, flexible skin on our lips is exposed to the air, as well as constantly moving and stretching during normal daily activities—for example, eating, talking, whistling, and kissing—it is essential to keep it moisturized and elastic. Here's how to make your own custom-flavored variety of protective lip balm.

- In a **small saucepan**, heat **3 tablespoons (45 mL) olive oil** and **1 tablespoon (15 mL) beeswax** until melted. Add **2 to 4 drops vanilla extract or essential oil of your choice (grapefruit, lemon, and spearmint** all work well) and stir to combine. Pour mixture into a **clean, resealable, wide-mouthed 2-ounce (60 mL) jar or tin** and allow to cool. If the balm is too hard at room temperature, re-melt and add a little more olive oil; if it is too soft, re-melt and add a little more beeswax.

Tooth-Whitening Pretreatment

The whiteness of teeth is determined by several factors: your genes, your diet (you knew all that black coffee and red wine was going to stain your chompers, right?), and your oral hygiene routine. Only two are factors you can control, and of those, your dental care regime is probably the easiest to change. (Give up the red wine, maybe. But coffee? Never.) This before-brushing mouthwash will work wonders **over the course of three months if used twice per day**.

NOTE: Give your teeth a **one-month break after three months** of treatment.

~~~~~~~~~

- In a **small saucepan**, heat **1 cup (250 mL) water** and **1 tablespoon (15 mL) salt** until the salt dissolves, then turn off the heat. In a **large bowl**, add ¼ cup (60 mL) loosely packed fresh spearmint leaves and pour the mixture over the leaves. Steep for **10 minutes**. Using a **funnel**, pour the water through a **fine-mesh stainless-steel strainer** into a **clean, resealable 16-ounce bottle** and add **1 cup (250 mL) hydrogen peroxide** and **1 tablespoon (15 mL) baking soda**. Allow to cool completely before capping the bottle.

- Before brushing in the morning and in the evening, swish **1 or 2 tablespoons (15 or 30 mL)** of this prewash around your mouth for **1 minute**, gargling before spitting out the rinse.

Whitening Toothpaste

Come for the whitening, stay for the antibacterial properties! This is a great, inexpensive preparation that does an excellent job at whitening teeth, fighting cavities, and controlling bad breath—plus, it's dentist-approved.

NOTE: Both salt and baking soda are effective against bacteria that cause cavities, but neither is as powerful as fluoride; use this preparation **no more than once per day**, alternating with your regular toothpaste.

- In a **small bowl**, add **2 or 3 fresh spearmint or sage leaves**, **1 teaspoon (5 mL) baking soda**, and **½ teaspoon (2.5 mL) sea salt**. With the back of a **spoon**, crush the powder into the herbs for a **few seconds** to release the scent, then remove the leaves. Add **1 teaspoon (5 mL) water** and mix to create a thick paste. Scoop the scented paste out of the bowl with your **toothbrush** and polish those pearly whites.

Mouthwash

When your brushing and flossing are done, it's time to rinse your mouth with something that will leave you with some ongoing protection against the bacteria that cause cavities and bad breath.

NOTE: Avoid mouthwashes that contain alcohol—it will only dry out the tissues in your mouth, increasing your chances of raising up a bumper crop of bad breath–causing bacteria.

- In a **large bowl**, mix **1 cup (250 mL) aloe vera juice**, **½ cup (125 mL) distilled water**, **2 teaspoons (10 mL) baking soda**, **5 drops sage essential oil**, and **5 drops spearmint essential oil** until the baking soda has dissolved. Using a **funnel**, pour the mixture into a **clean 16-ounce (500 mL) bottle**. Swish **1 or 2 tablespoons (15 or 30 mL)** around your **mouth** for **1 minute**, gargling before spitting out the mouthwash.

Retainer Maintainer

Wearing braces is a traumatic experience for most of us, leading to all sorts of irrational fears of dentists, orthodontists, and their sinister co-conspirators, oral hygienists. But when those teeth emerged all straight and perfectly aligned, it sure felt great, right? To make sure your teeth stay properly aligned and never need braces again, you must use your retainer—and if you use a retainer, you need to care for it properly.

STORING RETAINERS

- The first rule of retainer club is never let the retainer dry out. In a **coffee mug or glass jar**, add **1 cup (250 mL) distilled water** and **1 teaspoon (5 mL) baking soda**, stirring until the baking soda dissolves. Store the retainer in this solution and rinse it with **cold water** before using.

CLEANING RETAINERS

- The second rule of retainer club is that you should give it a warm, cleansing bath **once per week**. In a **small bowl**, dissolve **1 teaspoon (5 mL) fine sea salt** in **1 cup (250 mL) warm water**. Add **1 tablespoon (15 mL) baking soda** and **1 tablespoon (15 mL) white vinegar**. Soak the retainer in this foaming mixture for **15 minutes**. Rinse with **cold water** before using or returning to storage.

Sore Throat Wash

When we're ill, and particularly when we're suffering from respiratory issues like coughing, sore throat, and lung congestion, gargling with salt water is a proven way to ease the discomfort and shorten the duration of the illness. Salt water soothes inflamed tissues and is antimicrobial to boot. While the cure for the common cold remains elusive, at least we can alleviate the symptoms.

• In a **12-ounce (375 mL) drinking glass**, mix **1 cup (250 mL) warm water** with **1 teaspoon (5 mL) fine sea salt**, stirring until the salt has dissolved. One mouthful at a time, gargle for **1 minute** and spit out the saline solution, repeating until the glass is empty. Repeat **3 times per day** when you are ill and you can shorten the duration of your symptoms by as much as **40 percent**.

Lemony Throat Soother

If you are suffering from a cold, chances are you also have a sore throat. Soothe it with a tonic that combines the antibacterial, antiviral, antioxidant, and immune system–boosting qualities of honey and lemon juice. Repeat this as often as necessary when you are sick.

● In a **large coffee mug**, mix **1 cup (250 mL) hot water**, **2 teaspoons (10 mL) freshly squeezed lemon juice**, and **1 teaspoon (5 mL) honey**. Sip this hot concoction, letting it soothe your throat as it goes down.

Canker Sore Reliever

Canker sores were the bane of my existence as a kid—in large part because I was a huge fan of orange juice, which is quite acidic. Food and beverages that are spicy or acidic can cause agony in the mouths of the afflicted—even mild food can irritate a canker sore just by touching it. To lower the acidity of your mouth, promote healing, and help ease the pain of eating, **use this rinse before every meal and after your last toothbrushing of the day until the sore heals**.

- In a **12-ounce (375 mL) drinking glass**, mix **1 cup (250 mL) warm water**, **1 teaspoon (5 mL) baking soda**, and **1 teaspoon (5 mL) salt**, stirring until everything has dissolved. Take a mouthful of this mixture before and after eating, swirling around your mouth for **1 minute** before spitting out the rinse.

Earache Soother

When I was practicing for my junior lifesaving certification, I spent a lot of time in the community pool pretending to drown or rescuing other kids who were pretending to drown. As a result, I had multiple cases of swimmer's ear every summer for a few years running. *Swimmer's ear*, I later learned, is a bit of a misnomer—tons of people who don't swim at all suffer from the condition, also known as *otitis externa*, which is a fancy name for an infection of the outer ear canal. If you have an earache, this remedy works wonders by removing ear wax, dirt, allergens, bacteria, and other gunk in your ear.

NOTE: If the pain worsens despite this treatment, you may need oral antibiotics—an untreated ear infection can lead to a ruptured eardrum, so be sure to consult a doctor.

• Using a **small funnel**, pour **2 tablespoons (30 mL) 70 percent isopropyl alcohol** and **2 tablespoons (30 mL) white vinegar** into a **clean 2-ounce (60 mL) glass dropper bottle**. Tilt your head to the side so your affected ear is facing up and, using the dropper, pour about **1 teaspoon (5 mL)** of this mixture into your ear canal, letting it sit for **1 minute**. Tilt the affected ear down and let the solution drain out. Thoroughly dry the ear canal with the corner of a **clean towel** or blow-dry your ear gently with a **hair dryer** on the lowest setting, held **1 foot (30 cm)** away from the side of your head. Repeat **3 times daily** until the earache subsides.

Nasal Irrigation Solution

The mucosal linings of our sinuses—so moist, so warm—are a perfect landing pad for airborne allergens, bacteria, and viruses, which can leave us with stuffy or blocked nasal passages. One proven way of easing nasal congestion or lessening the symptoms of an allergy attack is nasal irrigation, an Ayurvedic practice called *jala neti* that dates back as far as five thousand years. It's even been shown to reduce the viral load in your sinuses when you are afflicted with a rhinovirus such as the common cold. The process involves pouring a saline solution into one nostril and letting it flow out the other, flushing out all the junk. It takes a little practice, but it is a worthwhile technique to learn.

- In a **small saucepan**, mix **2 cups (500 mL) water** and **1 tablespoon (15 mL) pure, non-iodized salt (or kosher salt with no additives)** and **boil** for a **minimum of 15 minutes**. Remove the pot from the heat and pour the solution into a **sterile, resealable 16-ounce (500 mL) glass jar**. Store at room temperature.

- To use, warm **1 cup (250 mL) of the solution** to just below body temperature and pour into a **neti pot or nasal irrigation bottle**. Standing over the sink, tilt your head to one side, insert the spout of the neti pot or bottle into the top nostril, and let about half the water trickle through. (You'll have to find the angle that allows the water to flow directly out of your bottom nostril without spilling into the back of your throat.) Tilt your head to the other side and repeat until the solution is gone. Tilt your head forward over the sink and snort any remaining water out. Then gently blow your nose a couple of times to completely drain the water. You can do this as many times as you wish until you can breathe more easily through your nose.

Eye Wash

If you have a foreign object stuck in your eye or a case of conjunctivitis (inflammation of the conjunctiva, the thin lining of the inner eyelid and white of your eye), your eye will appear bloodshot and will itch or feel uncomfortable. This simple saline solution is a good option for rinsing away foreign objects or bacteria and easing any discomfort.

- In a **small saucepan**, mix **2 cups (500 mL) water** and **1 teaspoon (5 mL) pure, non-iodized salt (or kosher salt with no additives)** and **boil** for a **minimum of 15 minutes**. Remove the pot from the heat and pour the solution into a **sterile, resealable 16-ounce (500 mL) glass jar**. Store at room temperature.

- To use, warm **½ cup (125 mL) of the solution** to just below body temperature and pour into a **small drinking glass**. Tilt your head back over the sink or bathtub and place the lip of the glass below your eye while holding your eyelids open with the fingers of your other hand. Carefully pour the water over the surface of your eye so it runs from the inner corner to the outer corner and down your cheek.

NOTE: If you have conjunctivitis and plan to clean both eyes, thoroughly wash your hands and the drinking glass before switching to your other eye—some forms of conjunctivitis are very contagious!

Eye Makeup Remover

When it comes time to remove makeup from around your eyes, this simple method not only safely removes any last traces, it also moisturizes the skin around your eyes and conditions your eyelashes.

● Lightly soak a **cotton ball** in **olive oil** and use it to very gently rub the makeup from around your eyes, working from the inner corners toward the outside corners and using a semicircular motion. Repeat with new cotton balls as necessary until the makeup is gone.

(Temporary) Tattoo Remover

It goes without saying, but this technique will not work on any ill-conceived and regrettable permanent skin art—if you're sporting ink you wish you didn't have, you'll need to see a trained professional to get rid of it. But if you have a *temporary* tattoo that has begun to flake and look more like an unpleasant skin condition than art, here's how to erase it.

- Take a **small handful of salt** and **a couple of drops of olive oil** and use it to rub away the temporary tattoo—since these tattoos are like decals, the salt crystals will scour away any lingering remnants from the surface of your skin. Wash and moisturize when you're done.

NOTE: It is possible to *lighten* henna tattoos with a **20- to 30-minute** topical application of **olive or coconut oil** to the affected skin, but this won't completely remove them—the molecules of the plant extract used in henna tattoos bind to the keratin in your skin and only disappear completely with the passage of time and the shedding of your epidermis.

Splinter Treatment

As a feral child who ran around barefoot as often as possible (especially during the summer when the very thought of shoes offended me), I got a lot of splinters in my hands and feet. If tweezers couldn't remove the splinters, the skin around them would sometimes become infected and painful, and they would have to be dug out, along with a chunk of skin. Here's a better way to remove these bitter barbs.

- Begin by soaking the area of skin with the splinter in **white vinegar** for **30 minutes**. The acid in the vinegar will help shrink the skin around the splinter, bringing it close enough to the surface to be grabbed with the **tweezers**.

- If that doesn't work, mix **½ teaspoon (2.5 mL) baking soda** with **a few drops of water** to create a paste. Spread the paste on the skin around the splinter and cover with a **sterile bandage**. Wait **24 hours** before removing the bandage, at which point the skin around the splinter should have pushed the splinter to the surface, allowing you to grab it.

Foot Scrub

The bottoms of your feet are just like the rest of your skin, just tougher and more jaded from being stuffed into shoes and walked on, day in and day out. To soften up those leathery soles, try this coarse scrub.

- In a **small bowl**, mix **2 tablespoons (30 mL) white vinegar**, **2 tablespoons (30 mL) honey**, and **2 tablespoons (30 mL) coarse sea salt**. Sitting on the edge of the bathtub, **vigorously scrub** the underside of one foot from heel to toes, focusing on the thickest areas of callused skin. Repeat with the other foot and rinse before moving on to the **Tropical Foot Soak (page 186)**.

Tropical Foot Soak

After scrubbing away the gnarliest skin from the bottoms of your feet **(Foot Scrub, page 185)**, it's time to soften the skin even more with a moisturizing soak born in the tropics.

● In a **blender or food processor**, place **2 ripe bananas**, **2 tablespoons (30 mL) freshly squeezed lemon juice**, **2 tablespoons (30 mL) fine sea salt**, and **1 tablespoon (15 mL) coconut oil**. Blend on **high** for **1 minute** and pour into a **medium bowl**.

● Sitting on the edge of the bathtub, coat your feet completely with this mixture and massage it into the skin. Wait **15 minutes** before rinsing the banana mash from your feet with **warm water**. Moisturize with **Body Lotion (page 155)**.

Athlete's Foot Treatment

The scourge of locker rooms everywhere, athlete's foot (or *tinea pedis*) is a flaky, itchy rash that can be quite painful, especially if it causes cracks in the skin. It is caused by a fungus that likes to hang out in the moist areas between the toes and spread from there.

NOTE: While you are treating athlete's foot, change your socks a few times per day, if possible, and keep your feet dry. Avoid wearing the same shoes two days in a row—better yet, avoid wearing shoes as much as possible.

~~~~~~~~~~

SALINE SOLUTION

- High concentrations of salt are lethal to microbes of all kinds, including the fungus that causes athlete's foot. Fill a shallow tub just large enough to fit both feet with **½ gallon (2 L) hot water** and pour in **1 cup (250 mL) fine sea salt**, stirring to dissolve. Soak your feet in this saline solution for **15 minutes once per day** until the condition improves. Dry your feet thoroughly.

HYDROGEN PEROXIDE

- Hydrogen peroxide is an excellent antifungal. Using a **cotton ball soaked in hydrogen peroxide**, apply it directly to the rash on your feet **two times per day**, until the condition improves. Rinse and dry your feet thoroughly after each application.

TEA TREE ESSENTIAL OIL

- Tea tree, another effective antifungal, is frequently used to treat both dandruff and athlete's foot. Using a **cotton pad**, apply **tea tree oil** directly to the rash on your feet **two times per day** until the condition improves.

Nail Polish Pretreatment

If you are one of those remarkable, steady-handed people who apply their own nail polish, here is a pre-application treatment that may well improve your efforts, no matter how skilled you've become as your own nail stylist.

- The first thing to do is to cut and shape your nails with **scissors or a nail clipper** while the nails are dry. File with an **emery board** after cutting.

- Next, soften the cuticles so they can be shaped without damaging them. In a **small bowl**, mix **½ cup (125 mL) water** and **½ cup (125 mL) white vinegar** and soak your fingertips in this mixture for **1 minute**. Using a **cuticle pusher**, gently shape your cuticles by pushing them back from the nail.

- It is essential to completely dry your nails before applying polish—remember this the next time you're at the salon. Any extra moisture causes them to expand a little, and if polish is applied before the nails shrink back to normal, it could cause the manicure to crack. Wait at least **30 minutes** after soaking before the last pretreatment step.

- Finally, using a **cotton swab**, apply **coconut oil** to the skin around the sides and bottom of each nail. This ensures that if you color outside the lines (that is, onto your skin) you can easily clean the excess without damaging the manicure once the polish on the nails has dried.

Heavy-Duty Hand Cleanser

Some substances in the world (I'm looking at you, bike grease) are very difficult to clean off with conventional soap. This treatment will cut through the toughest grime and exfoliate your hands at the same time.

- In a **small bowl**, mix **1 tablespoon (15 mL) apple cider vinegar** and **1 tablespoon (15 mL) cornmeal**. Scoop a little of this loose paste into your hands and scrub the trouble areas. Reapply until the grime is gone. Rinse under **warm water** and moisturize using a dab of **Body Lotion (page 155)**.

Rash Treatment

Bad rashes happen to good people, and for all sorts of reasons: allergies, infections, excessive heat, parasites (sorry but it's true), immune disorders, and so on. Depending on the type of rash, different treatments exist to treat the underlying cause, but there is one home remedy that works to soothe the itchy discomfort caused by all of them.

NOTE: **If a painful rash persists for more than a few days, consult a doctor.**

- In a **blender or food processor**, blend **1 cup (250 mL) old-fashioned rolled oats** until the oats turn into a fine powder. Add **1 cup (250 mL) baking soda** to the powdered oats and pulse to combine. Draw a **warm bath**—hot water exacerbates most rashes—and pour in the powdered oats mixture. Soak in the bath for up to **40 minutes**.

NOTE: If you are bathing a baby with diaper rash, add **2 teaspoons (10 mL) powdered oats** and **2 teaspoons (10 mL) baking soda** to **lukewarm water** in the **baby bathtub** and stir to combine. Repeat **twice daily** until the rash subsides.

Sunburn Soother

If you spend any time in the sun, always wear sunscreen, even if you have dark skin—ultraviolet radiation is an equal-opportunity scorcher and the burning begins after only ten minutes of direct exposure. The best sunscreens contain a physical barrier (titanium dioxide or zinc oxide), whereas chemical sun-blocking sunscreens frequently contain harmful chemicals that can leach into the bloodstream and don't even last very long before you have to reapply. But if you do miss a spot before heading out for a day in the sun, here's how to treat the inevitable burn.

- In a **medium bowl**, mix **½ cup (125 mL) aloe vera gel**, **¼ cup (60 mL) whipped coconut oil** (follow the instructions for **Body Lotion, page 155**), **1 tablespoon (15 mL) olive oil**, **3 drops lavender essential oil**, and **3 drops eucalyptus essential oil**.

- Next, **take a cool shower or bath**—the burn will immediately start to dry out your skin, so keeping it moist and cool will make you more comfortable. Do not rub yourself dry with a **towel**—instead, use it to pat your skin almost dry, making sure to leave a little moisture on the surface. Trap the moisture against your skin by immediately applying the aloe vera moisturizer to any affected area.

- Finally, drink lots of water while your burn is healing to replace the extra water your body is using to repair your dry, damaged skin.

Muscle Ache Soother

After a strenuous workout, whether at the gym, during a big grocery shop, playing with little kids, or sneezing wrong (it happens!), our muscles get sore. Here's a simple balm that relies on the power of essential oils to soothe aching muscles.

~~~~~~~~

- In a **small, microwave-safe bowl**, add **1 teaspoon (5 mL) beeswax**, **1 tablespoon (15 mL) coconut oil**, and **1 teaspoon (5 mL) olive oil**. Heat for **5 seconds on high power** to melt; return to **microwave** for a **few more seconds** if necessary. Stir to combine and allow the mixture to cool for **5 minutes**. Add **5 drops rosemary essential oil**, **5 drops peppermint essential oil**, and **5 drops lavender essential oil** and stir to thoroughly combine. Before the balm sets, pour into a **clean, resealable, wide-mouthed 2-ounce (30 mL) glass jar or storage tin**. To use, apply the balm with your fingertips to the affected muscles.

NOTE: Like many such remedies, the massaging works best when administered by a trusted (perhaps even beloved?) second party.

Indigestion Relief

Often connected to overindulgence at mealtime, dyspepsia (the ten-dollar word for indigestion) is a feeling of discomfort in the abdomen. It happens to lots of people, and the causes for it can include any number of factors, from diet (overeating, spicy foods) to personal habits (running, wearing too-tight pants, bending over after eating) to disease (ulcers, for example). For most forms of mild indigestion, this simple tea will soothe the savage stomach, but **if the pain persists or returns for more than a week or two, be sure to consult a doctor**.

- In a **coffee mug**, grate a **1-inch (2.5 cm) knob of peeled fresh ginger**. Add **1 teaspoon (5 mL) honey** and **½ teaspoon (2.5 mL) baking soda**, and top off with **warm water**. Stir to combine and slowly sip as the mixture cools.

NOTE: Baking soda is a base and will help neutralize the acid in the stomach, while ginger is clinically proven to soothe an upset stomach and curb nausea.

CHAPTER 8

THE ANIMAL KINGDOM

On the short list of the most delightful roommates with whom I've ever had the pleasure of sharing the domestic sphere, several pets I've known over the years take some of the top spots. Whether hamsters, birds, cats, dogs, they were (mostly) all excellent companions—loving, filled with personality, and best of all, rarely (if ever) short-tempered or cross. On the downside, pets add a substantial layer of responsibility to our lives and force us to make lots of accommodations. Not only do they leave their waste lying around for us to clean up, pets also rely on us to provide them with absolutely everything in their lives, from entertainment and food to shelter and health care. (And deworming. Did I mention deworming?) The recipes in this chapter are suggestions for ways in which you can make your pets' lives that much better, providing healthy, all-natural solutions to some of the challenges they (and you) face.

NOTE: With sincere apologies to fans of other species as life companions, this chapter focuses on dogs and cats.

Dog Shampoo and Rinse

Dogs get dirty. Really dirty. And smelly. And they love it. You know what else they get? Fleas, ticks, and other bloodsuckers that lurk in the grass, waiting for snuffling dogs to wander by. This shampoo is good for getting rid of dirt, odors, and biting insects (many of which don't like the smell of rosemary). And it's very mild, making it safe for dogs with sensitive skin.

NOTE: Test for potential allergic reactions by rubbing a small amount of the shampoo on a section of relatively hairless skin, rinsing, and waiting **5 minutes**. If there is no irritation visible, it should be fine.

- In a **small saucepan**, bring **1 cup (250 mL) water** to a **boil** and add **8 sprigs fresh rosemary**.

- While the rosemary-water cools, in a **clean 16-ounce (500 mL) glass spray bottle**, add **1 cup (250 mL) distilled water**, **¼ cup (60 mL) Castile soap**, **2 tablespoons (30 mL) apple cider vinegar**, and **2 tablespoons (30 mL) fresh lemon juice**. With your dog standing in the bath, dampen the fur and liberally spray the shampoo over every inch of its body (but not the head), including in the creases between the torso and limbs. Work the shampoo into the fur with your fingers and wait for **10 minutes**. Rinse thoroughly with **warm water**. Give a final rinse with the rosemary-water, working it into the dog's entire coat. Towel dry.

- If your dog absolutely hates taking a bath, try a dry shampoo treatment. In a **small bowl**, mix **1 cup (250 mL) baking soda**, **½ cup (125 mL) cornstarch**, and **5 drops rosemary essential oil**. Using a **flour sifter or fine-mesh stainless-steel strainer**, sprinkle the powder over your dog's coat and work it into the entire coat with your fingers or a **wide-toothed comb**.

Cat Shampoo

You could, in theory, wash your cats. Every now and then, you come across eyewitness accounts—videos, even—of this remarkable feat. But cats are generally not agreeable to the notion, and you could get injured in the attempt. (You come across video evidence of *that* all the time.) On the plus side, cats take pretty good care of cleaning themselves—cat saliva may just be the best all-natural cat shampoo. (Which makes sense, since cat skin is notoriously sensitive.)

- If your cat is an outdoor traveler and has a flea problem—or if it has been sprayed by a skunk—I recommend taking your feline companion to a professional, who will be equipped with the appropriate body armor the job of cat-washing requires. But if you're feeling brave, or desperate, find a human accomplice, grab a couple **oven mitts**, lock yourselves and your cat into the bathroom, and rinse your cat in the tub with **lukewarm water** while your partner does their best to hold the cat in place.

NOTE: Prepare to get serious side-eye from your cat for the rest of the day, and possibly for an entire week.

Pet Bed Deodorizer

If your pet's bed is too big to fit inside your washing machine, don't despair—you can remove that sweaty, hot-under-the-saddle, straight-out-of-the-jungle animal funk without upsetting your pet's delicate sensibilities or putting undue stress on the cleaning equipment. As always with odor-eating solutions, the hero of this story is baking soda.

- First, **vacuum** your pet's **bed** to remove hair and dander (the polite word for skin flakes). Then, using a **flour sifter or fine-mesh stainless-steel strainer**, sprinkle **baking soda** all over the surface of the pet bed and let it sit for at least **3 hours**, but **preferably overnight**, making sure your pet does not have access to the bed during that time. Vacuum thoroughly and return the bed to your pet.

NOTE: **Do not** use scented baking soda for this application—animal skin can be quite sensitive, and some essential oils (especially tea tree oil) can irritate or, even in rare instances, prove fatal to some pets.

Flea-Proofing Cat and Dog Beds and Rugs

If you or I were to discover our skin was covered by parasitic insects feeding on our blood, we'd do something about it. But aside from vigorous scratching, our pets' attitudes to such infestations is very live-and-let-live. Since your pets can't take care of the problem (and since those bloodsuckers might move on to your skin if left unchecked), here's how you can help keep fleas at bay.

- First, wash your pet (**Dog Shampoo and Rinse, page 196**, or **Cat Shampoo, page 197**).

- While your pet is tearing around the house, air-drying, **vacuum** everywhere, especially cracks and corners where fleas like to lay eggs. Daily vacuuming is one of the most effective home remedies against fleas.

- Next, thoroughly clean the pet's **bed** and other preferred sleeping areas (if the latter category includes your bed, your **mattress** needs to be **vacuumed and washed** and your bed linens need to be thoroughly cleaned in **hot water**). In a **small bowl**, mix **1 cup (250 mL) baking soda** and **1 cup (250 mL) fine salt**. Using a **flour sifter or fine-mesh stainless-steel strainer**, liberally sprinkle this mixture over the pet's bed and allow to sit for at least **3 hours**, preferably overnight, before vacuuming again. The goal here is to dehydrate the fleas and flea eggs in the fabric. If you want to clean all the rugs and carpets in your home, scale up this recipe.

- Finally, wash those beds and carpets, either in the **washing machine** on the **hot cycle** (if they fit) or where they are, using **Rug and Carpet Shampoo (page 62)**. Until the fleas are eliminated, you may need to repeat these steps **every couple of days**—and keep your pets out of your bed until the fleas are gone!

Puppy Pee Preventer and Anti-Chew Spray

Like human babies, puppies need to learn how to control their bladders. But while you wait for that blessed level of self-control to arrive, you can discourage your puppy from peeing in certain areas by spraying floors and carpets with this concoction.

- Mix **1 part white vinegar** to **1 part water** in a **clean 8-ounce (250 mL) glass spray bottle**. Replace the spray nozzle and spray on the areas you'd like to discourage your pet from peeing on. If your puppy has an accident on your carpet anyways, see **Rug and Carpet Stain Cleaner (page 65)** for next steps.

- This spray also works to discourage your puppy from chewing on things it really shouldn't. If you can't move the objects of your puppy's affection into a closet or other protected space, spray them with this vinegar-water spray.

Cat-Scratch Deterrent

One of the more regrettable habits cats have is working out their nail care issues on the furniture. To prevent them from ripping up your sofas and club chairs, try spraying the areas your cats are attracted to with this spray.

- In a **small saucepan**, bring **1 cup (250 mL) water** to a **boil** and add **8 sprigs fresh rosemary**. While the rosemary-water cools, use a **small funnel** to pour **1 cup (250 mL) apple cider vinegar** and **¼ cup (60 mL) Castile soap** into a **clean 16-ounce (500 mL) glass spray bottle**. Add enough rosemary-water to fill the bottle and replace the spray nozzle. Gently swirl the mixture to combine (you don't want to agitate the soap or it will foam) and lightly spray any of your cat's preferred shredding zones.

Dog Crate and Cat Carrier Cleaner

If your dog or cat loses control of its bladder or bowels inside its crate or carrier, it's important to clean it right away or your pet will be much less agreeable the next time you invite them to step inside.

- Remove any **bedding** and clean in the **washing machine**. Next, spray the **floor of the crate or carrier** with a **clean 8-ounce (250 mL) glass spray bottle** filled with **white vinegar**. Wait **10 minutes** and mop up the dried vinegar with a **clean, damp sponge**. Thoroughly dry with a **clean rag** and, using a **flour sifter or fine-mesh stainless-steel strainer**, sprinkle the floor with a light coating of **baking soda** before replacing the pet bedding.

Paw Pad Protector

If your dog is an all-weather animal and loves to go outside in winter (especially when it snows), pay attention to the paw pads. Between the hard ground, the ice, and the salt used to melt the snow, your dog's paws can become raw and cracked. To both prevent this from happening and to treat the discomfort if it does happen, try this.

~~~~~~~~

- Thoroughly rub **olive oil** or **coconut oil** into your dog's pads before and after any trip outside into the cold.

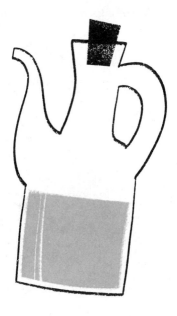

Hairball Preventer

Hairballs (or *trichobezoars*, as they're also known) are going to happen no matter what you do. Because cats do such an efficient job cleaning themselves with their Velcro-like tongues, their digestive tracts regularly fill with hair. And when that hair needs to come out, your cat will start convulsing and retching and cough up a slimy log. (It is an unpleasant habit, but totally normal and far better than the alternative: some cats have trouble regurgitating this hair mass, which can grow inside the stomach to such proportions that it needs to be removed surgically.)

~~~~~~~~~~

- To lessen the frequency of hairball expulsion (and the likelihood of a life-threatening ball of hair accumulating in your cat's gut), mix **1 teaspoon (5 mL) olive oil** into their food **once per week**.

Litter Box Cleanser

Because cats are apex predators—or at least, the distant relatives of desert-living apex predators—they have many fascinating qualities. They are skilled hunters, they have remarkable eyesight and can see in the dark, they are capable of jumping several times their height from a standing position, can run at speeds above twenty miles (thirty-two kilometers) per hour in short bursts, and they have the long, dagger-like teeth of a carnivore. And because of their desert heritage, cats rely almost entirely on what they eat for moisture—their bodies have evolved to be very efficient in their use of water, which is why you rarely see cats drink (unless they eat an all-kibble diet). Alas, this means that their urine is incredibly concentrated. And smelly: as bacteria break down the concentrated urea in the cat's urine, one of the by-products is ammonia. For this reason, it's critical for your cat's quality of life (and yours) to **scoop the litter daily, add clean litter every few days, and give the litter box itself a good cleaning every two to four weeks**.

- Using a **small funnel**, pour **½ cup (125 mL) white vinegar**, **1 tablespoon (15 mL) Castile soap**, and **1½ cups (375 mL) water** into a **clean 16-ounce (500 mL) glass spray bottle**. Replace the nozzle and gently swirl the contents to combine (you don't want to agitate the soap too much or it will foam).

- Wearing **rubber or latex gloves**, empty the **litter box** into a **garbage bag** and thoroughly spray the interior with the litter box cleanser. Thoroughly mop up the box with a **clean, damp sponge** until all the litter powder and cleanser are gone and the box is odor-free. Dry thoroughly and sprinkle the bottom of the litter box with **baking soda** before refilling with a fresh batch of litter.

NOTE: Sprinkle the bottom of the box with baking soda any time you change the litter to help control odors.

CHAPTER 9

THE GREAT OUTDOORS

Having an outdoor space to call one's own is undeniably a blessing, one that countless city dwellers envy. For while it's true that an urban lifestyle provides many social and cultural perks, the biggest sacrifice is the inhabitants' inability to experience nature whenever they want. With a growing body of research showing that exposure to greenery, and to trees in particular, is beneficial to mental and physical well-being, it is no wonder that city planners around the world are trying to figure out ways to bring more plants and trees into the urban setting. Plus if you have outdoor space, you probably also have your own garage or parking spot too. So if you are one of the people lucky enough to have outdoor space to call your own—whether it's a backyard, terrace, patio, porch, or neighborhood vegetable patch—the rest of us salute you (and, by the way, wonder when you're going to invite us over for a backyard barbecue). This chapter, which contains suggestions for cleaning, tidying, and maintaining your "outdoor rooms" using all-natural ingredients, should give you all sorts of reasons to spend more time in the great outdoors.

Red-Brick Cleanser

The use of bricks—compacted blocks of dried clay, sand, ash, and other minerals (including iron oxide, which gives red brick its color)—is nearly as old as human habitation itself, dating back to around 5000 BCE. Many ancient civilizations, including the Egyptians, used bricks made of clay and straw that were dried in the sun to build their cities. One of the great strides in the manufacturing of this now-standard building material was the innovation, around 3500 BCE, of firing the bricks in a kiln to harden them, making them even stronger. This led to widespread adoption of the brick as a building material, with the civil engineers of the Roman Empire spreading its use throughout central and western Europe. Today bricks are still used around the world in countless building projects. As durable and beautiful as a red-brick fireplace, wall, or patio is, though, it still needs to be cleaned regularly.

● In a **large bucket**, mix **1 gallon (4 L) water** with **½ gallon (2 L) white vinegar**. Using a **clean sponge mop**, spread this vinegar-water mixture across the surface of the **bricks**. Wait **10 minutes** and then scrub the surface with a **stiff, long-handled brush**.

Teak Furniture Reviver

If you have untreated outdoor furniture made of teak or another close-grained hardwood, it is important to clean and reseal the surface **once a year** to maintain its resilience to the elements. Treated with care, hardwood furniture will last for many years.

~~~~~~~~~

● Remove any upholstered items from the furniture. Using the **scouring side of a sponge**, begin by cleaning the surface of the **hardwood furniture** with a mixture of **1 gallon (4 L) warm water** and **1 tablespoon (15 mL) liquid Castile soap**. When the surface is completely dry, use a **sanding block wrapped with fine-grit sandpaper** to gently scrape away the gray surface of the wood, exposing the golden wood beneath.

● Using a **small funnel**, pour **2 cups (500 mL) grapeseed oil** and **1 cup (250 mL) white vinegar** into a **clean 1-quart (1 L) spray bottle**. Replace the spray nozzle, then shake the contents and squirt the mixture onto the surface of the wood. Give the bottle a shake after every second or third squirt to keep the mixture from separating, spraying until the furniture has been covered. Wait for **10 minutes**, then mop up any excess sealant with a **clean, dry rag**.

Barbecue Grill Cleanser

Though nothing symbolizes the warmer months of the year like the smell of barbecue wafting through the air, lots of home cooks use their grills year-round. If you frequently prepare meals on your barbecue, you know the importance of keeping the racks as clean as possible (just as you probably also know that it is not safe to scrape the grills with a wire brush—small bits of wire can break off and become lodged in the food you cook next).

- In a **clean 16-ounce (500 mL) glass spray bottle**, mix **1 cup (250 mL) water** and **1 cup (250 mL) white vinegar**. Replace the spray nozzle and shake well.

- Remove the greasy **cooking grates** from the grill and lay them on top of **flattened-out cardboard or newspaper**. Sprinkle the grates liberally with **baking soda** on both sides. Spray the grill with the water-vinegar spray until the baking soda begins to foam. Wait **10 minutes** before using a **balled-up sheet of aluminum foil** to scrub both sides of the grates. Using a **clean rag**, wipe any remaining grime and moisture off the grates. Apply **grapeseed or canola oil** to both sides of the grates with a **paper towel or rag** to season.

Driveway and Garage Oil Stain Remover

As any automobile owner knows, many of the fluids that enable these modern conveyances to run are petroleum-based, which means they are greasy. And since cars (like the people who drive them) occasionally leak fluids, your driveway or garage is likely to bear the brunt of these leaks. If you notice an oil stain, use this technique to clean it up immediately—the sooner you address such a spill, the more likely you will prevent it from becoming a permanent feature.

~~~~~~~~

- In a **medium bowl**, mix **1 cup (250 mL) salt** and **1 cup (250 mL) baking soda**. Spread this mixture liberally over the stain. Wait **10 minutes**.

- While the baking soda is absorbing some of the stain, fill **one bucket** with **1 gallon (4 L) white vinegar** and a **second bucket** with **1 gallon (4 L) hot water**. Dip the end of a **stiff, long-handled brush** into the vinegar and scrub at the stain, reapplying frequently. When the paste stops foaming, dip the brush into the water and scrub the stain clean, reapplying as necessary. Rinse away the grime with a **hose**.

Car Deodorizer

According to the latest research, the US market for car air fresheners (including aerosols, sprays, gels, and the little pine tree cutouts that dangle from the rearview mirror) is estimated to be around $240 million. If this eye-watering number tells us anything, it's that our cars must smell pretty good despite all the traveling, sweating, eating, and (occasionally) sleeping we do in them. But there's no reason to buy a commercial product made with chemicals that aren't that good for your health (and may cause actual distress to people with respiratory issues) when you can custom-make your own from natural ingredients for far less than what you'd pay at the gas-station convenience store.

- Remove any **mats** from your car and place them on the ground, preferably in **sunshine** (which is powerfully antibacterial). Liberally sprinkle the mats with **baking soda** while you tackle the rest of the car. If you'd like to add a scent to the car, add **10 to 20 drops essential oil of your choice** to every **1 cup (250 mL) baking soda** before sprinkling.

- Clean the trash from the floors, under the seats, and in any of the side pockets of the doors before thoroughly **vacuuming** the interior of the car, including the seats. Sprinkle a light dusting of **baking soda** on the **floor** and the **seats**. If you'd like to add a scent, add **10 to 20 drops essential oil of your choice** to the baking soda before sprinkling.

- Using the **All-Purpose Cleanser (page 18)**, spray the **dashboard** and inside surfaces of all the **windows** in the car. Using a **clean, lint-free cloth** dipped in a **bucket of clean warm water**, rub the dashboard and windows clean of any residue.

- Vacuum the baking soda off the floor and seats of the car. Vacuum the mats and place them back inside the car.

Windshield Wiper Blade Cleaner

It is alarming when you turn on the windshield wipers while driving in the middle of a rainstorm, only to find that the wipers can't clear the water from the glass well enough for you to see through it. To keep your wipers in working order, clean and condition them **every four to six weeks**.

~~~~~~~~~

● Lift the **wiper arms** up from windshield and check for cracks or splits in the rubber blades; if you see that kind of damage, they need to be replaced.

● If the blades are just dirty, pour some **white vinegar** onto a **clean, lint-free cloth** and gently but firmly rub the cloth up and down the length of each wiper blade, reapplying vinegar to a clean section of the cloth and wiping again until it stops leaving dirty residue behind. Once the blades are clean, put a few drops of **olive oil** onto a clean section of the cloth and rub up and down the length of the blade, reapplying as necessary. This is to "seal" the rubber and keep it from drying out (and squeaking). Wait for **10 minutes**.

● While the olive oil is soaking into the wiper blade, clean the windshield glass using **All-Purpose Glass Cleaner (page 70)** and **vacuum** the channel below the windshield to remove any leaves, branches, or other debris.

● When the 10 minutes are up, run a clean section of the cloth up and down the blades one last time to remove any excess olive oil. Place the wiper blades back against the windshield.

Chewing Gum Remover

If the sidewalk in front of your home or the driveway has been "decorated" with unsightly squidges of gum, try removing them with these two straightforward techniques.

FRESH GUM

- If the gum splotch is of recent vintage, the easiest thing to do is freeze it into submission. If the sun is out, set up an open **umbrella** to cast shade over the **gum**. Fill a **plastic bag with ice**, seal it, and place it on top of the gum. After about **15 minutes**, the gum should be a solid mass that can be easily dislodged from the ground with a **spackling blade** or other **metal scraper**. If not, give the ice a few minutes longer to turn that gum into a hard chip.

O.G. GUM

- If the sidewalk or driveway is covered in blackened, hardened discs of ancient gum, removing them will take a little more work. In a small bowl, mix **1 tablespoon (15 mL) baking soda**, **1 tablespoon (15 mL) coarse salt**, and **1 tablespoon (15 mL) cornmeal**. Spoon a small mound of this mixture over each disc of gum and sprinkle with **white vinegar**. As the mixture foams, use a **wire brush** to scrape the scouring mixture across the surface of the old **gum**. Repeat as necessary until all the fragments come up.

Sidewalk De-Icer

One of the remarkable qualities of salt is that it lowers the boiling point and freezing point of water. In cold climates, this handy feature means salt can be used to treat sidewalks and pathways that have become coated in ice (though at ambient temperatures below around 15 degrees F, or –9 degrees C, the ice won't melt). The larger the salt crystal, the better—even if the ice *doesn't* melt, the large chunks of salt will add texture to an otherwise frictionless surface, making it less slippery and safer to walk across.

- Fill a **large bucket** with **rock salt** (also known as *halite*, the mined form of salt, which contains many other trace minerals and can come in a variety of hues) or **coarse kosher salt** (the refined version of halite) and scatter handfuls of it across the walkway you are treating. In minutes, you will see the effects of the salt, weakening the ice and causing it to melt. This will make it much easier to chop the ice and scatter it to the side.

- If you need to clear the ice more quickly, fill a **large bucket** with **1 part rock or coarse kosher salt** and **3 parts boiling water**, stirring to combine. Pour this boiling saline solution over the ice you are removing from your walkway. Chop and scatter the remaining ice.

Mosquito Repellent

The most common ingredient in commercial insect repellents is the chemical known as DEET (or diethyltoluamide), developed by USDA scientist Samuel Gertler in 1944 to help the US Army slow the spread of insect-borne diseases that had proven deadly to American troops operating in the Pacific theater. DEET is effective but controversial: some studies have shown it to be toxic while others suggest it is perfectly safe when used properly. But all the warning labels say not to wear it under clothing and to keep it away from infants and young children, so why take the risk when there are other effective, all-natural ingredients that keep blood-sucking insects from feasting on your flesh?

- In a **clean, resealable 16-ounce (500 mL) glass jar**, add the **peels of 4 lemons** and pound into the bottom of the jar with a **long-handled wooden spoon** to release the fragrant oils. Add **1 cup (250 mL) 70 percent isopropyl alcohol** (or enough to cover) and seal the jar. Store the jar at room temperature for **2 weeks**, then strain the lemon peel–infused alcohol into a **clean 8-ounce glass jar**.

- Using a **small funnel**, pour **1 cup (250 mL) witch hazel**, ½ cup **(125 mL) lemon peel–infused alcohol**, and **50 drops citronella essential oil** into a **clean 16-ounce (500 mL) glass spray bottle**. Replace the spray nozzle and shake well before every use.

All-Natural Weed Killer

Whether growing between the pavers of your patio or among the vegetables in your kitchen garden, weeds are the unwanted guests of the plant world. They can cause damage to physical structures and choke out the plants you are actively trying to grow. Their persistence, however, is a testament to nature's endurance. But all green things can be torn from the earth or sent on to meet their maker by other means.

NOTE: With this spray, you hold the power of life and death in your hands—use it wisely, because it will wipe out any plant you spray with it and diminish the fertility of the soil into which it soaks.

● In a **large bowl**, mix **3 cups (750 mL) white vinegar**, **3 tablespoons (45 mL) fine salt**, and **1 teaspoon (5 mL) Castile soap**. Stir until the salt dissolves and, using a **funnel**, pour into a **clean 32-ounce (1 L) spray bottle**. Replace the spray nozzle and shake well. Spritz this solution directly onto the **plant** you are trying to kill, shielding the plants you want to spare with a piece of **cardboard** when you do. Within a week, the sprayed plants should be dead.

Ant Remediation

Although this recipe appears in the outdoors chapter, it is really for the benefit of the indoor environment. Ants are remarkable creatures, capable of incredible group and individual feats despite their small stature and minuscule brains (which contain a scant 250,000 neurons to the roughly 86 billion in our brains). They are also prolific breeders and tireless workers, with a knack for home invasion. These instructions—which include a nontoxic method of disrupting these insects' reliance on chemical signals, called *pheromones*, to navigate in the world and take advantage of their fondness for sugar—amount to a holistic approach to keeping them outside your home.

NOTE: This remediation program works on so-called sugar ants, the several species of tiny, sugar-loving ants commonly found in homes everywhere. If you have an infestation of carpenter ants or other destructive species, call an exterminator immediately.

- First, find where the ants are getting into the house by patiently observing them as they go about their business. Also try to discover where their nest is by following them *away* from the house—it won't be far. Finally, repeat the sleuthing process inside the house to see where they are coming in.

OUTDOOR CONTROL

- In a **small bowl**, mix ¼ cup (60 mL) cinnamon powder and ¼ cup **(60 mL) cayenne pepper** (both of which ants dislike); use this 1:1 ratio to make more, if needed. Sprinkle this mixture in a pencil-width line across the edge of the house where the ants are coming in—the longer the line, the better, since ants have infinite patience and will eventually find a way around any obstacle. The best barrier would go *all the way around the house*. And even that might not do it.

Finally, if you've found the nest, take the ultimate step of wiping out the colony. In a **large pot, boil 1 gallon (4 L) water** and slowly pour it into the **hole of the anthill or nest**. This will kill most of the ants inside as well as their eggs. Repeat as necessary.

NOTE: It will take a long time for the ants to return, but have no doubt—they'll be back, even if you do manage to take out the queen in the deluge.

INDOOR CONTROL

In a **small bowl, mix ¼ cup (60 mL) confectioners' sugar** and **¼ cup (60 mL) baking soda**. Place in **jar lids or other shallow containers** along the path the ants travel inside the house. They will take the laced sugar, a preferred food source, and bring it back to the nest. When ingested, baking soda (a base) reacts with the formic acid in an ant's digestive system to produce several by-products, including water and carbon dioxide, the latter of which will kill them.

Slug Trap

As any gardener knows, slugs can do immense damage in a garden—they may be slimy, slow-moving tubes of mucus, but that doesn't mean they don't get hungry. If you're tired of having your tenderest lettuces, herbs, and low-lying decorative plants devoured overnight, here's one way to take a stand. Special thanks to Patrick Dolan and Barbara Pleasant for this genius trap design and bait mixture.

● First, construct the physical trap. Using a **permanent marker**, draw a **line around the diameter** of a **1-quart (1 L) plastic takeout container (or other 1-quart plastic container with lid)**, about **2 inches (5 cm)** from the bottom. This is the baseline for the holes that will allow the slugs to enter the container. With a **sharp paring knife and scissors**, cut **four rectangular holes** in the container—each one should be about ½ inch (13 mm) high and 1½ inches (38 mm) wide, evenly spaced along the line you drew around the container.

● In a **small bowl**, mix **1 cup (250 mL) water, 1 teaspoon (5 mL) sugar, 1 teaspoon (5 mL) white flour**, and ½ teaspoon (2.5 mL) **dry yeast**. Pour the mixture into a **clean, resealable jar** and give it a good shake to combine. This bait takes advantage of slugs' fondness for carbohydrates and yeast (which is why beer is often used as bait).

● Bury the trap in a hole in the soil of your garden, but only up to the line you drew around the container—the slugs need to be able to slip into the holes you cut at soil level. Fill the bottom of the container with the bait, to just below the windows. Replace the lid of the trap (this will protect the bait from rain). Check the trap in **two days**—by then it will either 1) be filled with dead slugs or 2) need to have the bait replaced (it gets pretty smelly as fermentation sets in).

Garden Tool Preserver

Because garden tools are used for poking around in wet soil—which is also filled with lots of different minerals—they are prone to rusting. A little iron oxide isn't going to harm the plants in your garden, but it will shorten the life of your tools.

● Rinse your **garden tools** with a **garden hose** and then dry them thoroughly. Pour a little **olive oil** onto a **clean rag** and spread the oil all over the metal parts of the tools, reapplying as necessary. When all the tools have a thin coating of oil, let them dry for **4 hours or overnight**.

Flowerpot Reviver

At first glance, last year's flowerpots look like they might no longer be suitable containers for living things. But it is easy to clean up the limescale and caked-on dirt that make them look so unappealing. Plus you'll also be getting rid of any leftover harmful organisms.

● Place a handful of **coarse salt** on a **clean, damp rag** and use it to scour the inside and outside of the **pot**, reapplying salt and **a few drops** of water as necessary. When the pot is clean, rinse thoroughly with **cold water**.

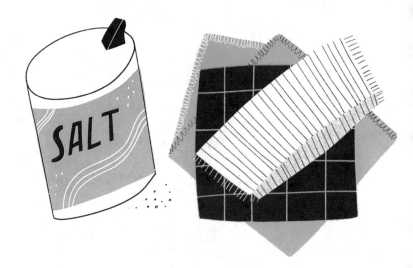

Do-It-Yourself Soil Analysis

Depending on what you want to plant in your garden, you are going to want to know a couple of important facts about the soil you'll be planting in. First, you'll want to know the composition of the soil—that is, the percentage of sand, silt, and clay. Next, you will need to know the pH level of the soil—is it alkaline (with a pH above 7), acidic (with a pH below 7), or neutral (pH of 7)? Most (but by no means all) plants grow in the slightly acidic range of 5.5 to 7 pH because this is the range favored by the microbes in the soil that help the plant's roots absorb nutrients most efficiently.

pH TEST

● Take **½ cup (125 mL) soil** from your garden, from a hole that's about **8 inches (20 cm) deep** (roughly where the taproots will be for most plants). Place half the soil in **one small bowl** and the other half in a **second small bowl**. Pour **¼ cup (60 mL) white vinegar** into the first bowl—if it fizzes, then the soil is alkaline. Pour **2 tablespoons (30 mL) water** into the second bowl and add **¼ cup (60 mL) baking soda**—if it fizzes, then the soil is acidic. And if neither fizzes, then the soil has a neutral pH. Consult the pH requirements of the plants you want to grow and take steps to adjust the soil accordingly.

NOTE: For a more exact measurement, invest in a digital pH-measuring tool.

SOIL COMPOSITION TEST

- Take ¾ cup (180 mL) soil from your garden, from a hole that's about **8 inches (20 cm) deep** (roughly where the taproots will be for most plants). Place the soil into a **clean, resealable 16-ounce (500 mL) glass jar** and fill the jar with water to a point **1 inch (2.5 cm) from the top** of the jar. Put the lid securely on the jar and shake vigorously. After **1 minute**, use a **ruler** to measure the height of the first layer to fall to the bottom, which is **sand.** After **90 minutes**, use the ruler to measure the next layer to settle, **silt**. After **48 hours**, use the **ruler** to measure the height of the top layer, **clay**, as well as the **total height** of the three layers combined. Divide the height of each layer by the total height to find the percentage of that layer. Consult the composition requirements for the plants you hope to grow and take steps to adjust the soil accordingly.

Rose, Tomato, and Pepper Booster

Although there is some controversy surrounding the practice of adding Epsom salt to soil—regular salt is, after all, poisonous to plants—countless gardeners have long maintained that you will get healthier, better fruiting and flowering rose, tomato, and pepper plants by using it. This is because all three use large amounts of magnesium and sulfur, particularly in the mid-to-late growing season, both of which are provided by Epsom salt (magnesium sulfate).

- At the beginning of the season, spoon **1 tablespoon (15 mL) Epsom salt** into the **planting holes**, whether you are putting seeds or transplants into the ground. Immediately **water** after planting to dissolve the salt and release its components into the soil.

- When leaves first begin to appear on the plants, or when new leaves start coming in on transplants, scatter **1 tablespoon (15 mL) Epsom salt** around the base of each plant **once every six weeks** until the end of the growing season. **Water** after every application.

- Later in the season, when fruits and flowers begin to come in, spray the **plants' leaves** (not the fruit or flowers) with an **Epsom solution**, in lieu of watering, **once per month** until the end of the growing season. In a **large bowl**, add **2 teaspoons (10 mL) Epsom salt** to **1 quart (1 L) water** and stir until the salt has dissolved. Using a **funnel**, pour into a **clean 32-ounce (1 L) spray bottle** and replace the spray nozzle. This will keep the leaves healthy throughout the season and enable the plants to improve their uptake of other essential nutrients necessary to produce large flowers and fruit.

Powdery Mildew Treatment

One of the most common afflictions in any garden, whether ornamental or edible, is the dreaded powdery mildew, a disease caused by several different species of fungi that attack a wide variety of plants. The gray, powdery mildew is instantly identifiable (and highly contagious) and appears on both the stems and leaves of infected plants. As the furry spores spread, the gray spots grow larger and will eventually damage the health of the plant. If you spot powdery mildew in your garden, immediately start using this solution to stop its spread—if it becomes well established, the best you can hope for is to control it, not eliminate it.

- In a **large bowl**, add **½ gallon (2 L) water**, **2 teaspoons (10 mL) baking soda**, **2 teaspoons (10 mL) olive oil**, and **2 teaspoons (10 mL) Castile soap** and gently stir to combine. Using a **large funnel**, pour into a **clean 64-ounce (2 L) pump sprayer** and replace the spray nozzle. **Once per week**, in the morning, spray every leaf and stem affected by the powdery mildew. Within a couple of weeks, the plants should begin to clear up (or at the very least, the spores should stop spreading).

A NOTE ON THE WAY OUT

As mentioned at the start of this book, the world we live in today would be unrecognizable to our relatives from one hundred years ago in many ways, including how we shop for our food and household goods. Though a common feature of the landscape today, the first supermarket—defined as a large store with a wide variety of food and non-food items—didn't come into existence until roughly 1930, when King Kullen (whose slogan was "Pile it high; sell it cheap") opened in the borough of Queens, New York. Before that, shoppers went to the general store to browse the relatively small selection of essential goods, supplementing that with trips to specialty stores and grocers (or even farms themselves).

Once the supermarket appeared, though, one-stop shopping was quickly adopted around North America and, eventually, around the world. As a result, thousands of global agricultural businesses and manufacturers had to figure out how to increase their output to keep all those miles of shelves stocked with goods, leading to innovations in supply chain management, shipping technology, and infrastructure. And now, of course, we have the online superstore, stocked with literally *everything*, a concept that would have seemed as likely in the early twentieth century as sending a spaceship hurtling into interstellar space (a feat accomplished by *Voyager 1* in 2012).

The drive to create the massive amount of product needed to fill those supermarket shelves sprang up in parallel with rapid and transformative advances in chemical and manufacturing technology, both of which were bent to the demands of retail. At the same time, there was a growing belief (fueled by the emerging practice of advertising) that these newly invented manufactured products were vastly superior to the old-fashioned ones of previous generations—that is, the ones that were closer to nature. The result was the creation of innumerable products to replace existing ones, including many used in household cleaning and personal care, with very little attention paid to potential side effects on our health and on the health of the environment. With climate change now a reality, and thanks to recent decades of detailed research into the harmful effects of many of these chemicals, we know so much more. And armed with that knowledge, we can begin to change our behavior.

One thing that hasn't changed in the past century (and probably for far longer than that) is our recognizably human desire to make the healthiest possible choices for ourselves and our loved ones. While it has become increasingly clear that it will take nation-size actions to effectively combat the most pressing existential challenge of our time (global climate change), we can at least control the number of toxins we release within our homes and put onto, and into, our bodies. And since human progress is powered by the engine of hope and shaped by our reliance on, and love for, community, there is every reason to believe that these small choices might influence others around us—even those in the seats of power—to make better choices too.

ACKNOWLEDGMENTS

Writing is a solitary endeavor involving endless days and nights spent in the company of one's thoughts, tapping away at the keyboard—and, in the case of the book you now hold in your hands, conducting low-grade science experiments on my kitchen counter—hoping all the while that what emerges will appeal to readers. But the writing process is just one of several steps necessary to publish a book, each of which depends on the expertise of many other people along the way. This is a grateful acknowledgment of the efforts of the talented professionals who did their part (and then some) to make my late-night ramblings make sense. It goes without saying that whatever gaffes remain in the pages of this book are here despite their efforts and are my responsibility entirely.

Sasquatch Books is home to a talented group of publishing professionals, and I am grateful to them all for making the writing of this book such a pleasure. In particular, I want to thank editorial director Jen Worick, whose calm wisdom was a beacon to me throughout the writing of the manuscript; production editor Bridget Sweet, who lived up to her surname even as she worked hard to keep me on schedule and sounding sane; copyeditor Steven Blaski, whose sharp-eyed read-through improved the book in every possible way; proofreader Michelle Gale, who swept through the final layouts and brought them to a new level of readability; designer Tony Ong, who created a beautiful package that elevated the book into an object; the production team, headed by director Liza Brice-Dahmen, without whom the trains (cargo ships?) would never have arrived on time or with the correct freight; the preternaturally good-natured Jenn Rudsit, who diligently kept after me for marketing materials; marketing director Nikki Sprinkle and her team, for positioning the book in the marketplace as irresistible in every way; and director of sales Jenny Abrami and the amazing Penguin Random House sales reps, for making sure the book made the final journey to your hands. If I've left anyone out, I apologize, but I promise it is for reasons of space rather than lack of gratitude.

At home here in Brooklyn, I would like to thank my partner S. for indulging my months-long efforts to find useful combinations of common pantry items—there were many times when we ran out of the staples during those hectic days of experimentation, but she never complained, even when a few iterations of the homemade dishwasher soap didn't quite perform as promised. Normally I would also thank my two teenagers, D. & D., for their forbearance throughout this process, but these days they are overwhelmingly consumed with social experiments of their own and don't notice a lot of what goes on around them in the domestic sphere. Instead I will just say that I look forward to talking to them again when they are in their late twenties and again available for such interaction. Our cats, meanwhile, were instrumental in creating many of the household problems this book aims to solve and I am grateful for their grudging support.

Finally, I benefited immensely from reading the work of several other pantry pirates during my research for this book and am immensely grateful to them for all their innovations in the burgeoning field of all-natural solutions to everyday domestic challenges. But I must give a special shoutout to the great and brilliant Laura Westdale, a collector of human wisdom of every kind (especially the domestic variety), whose constant encouragement got me started on this project and saw me through to the end.

INDEX

ABOUT THE AUTHOR

Benjamin Mott is a professional cook, recipe tester, and editor with three decades of experience in nonfiction and cookbook publishing. Based in New York City, he has focused his food practice on farm-to-table cooking and organic food choices for more than two decades. And as a loving partner, a mindful parent of two children, and a steward of two very hairy cats, he came to appreciate the health benefits and awesome cleaning properties of many natural, nontoxic ingredients, adapting them for use in his own home.